Recovery for Everyone: Book
© 2014 by Douglas W. Weiss, Ph.D.
Discovery Press

Requests for information:
Discovery Press
heart2heart@xc.org
719-278-3708

Printed in the United States of America
ISBN #978-1-881292-13-5

Interior and Cover Design By: Janelle Evangelides
Edited By: Christianwriterhelp.com

Contents

Introduction

In the later 1980s, I can remember going to two conferences where they were training leaders at the Crystal Cathedral regarding starting recovery groups. That was more than twenty-five years ago.

It's been exciting to watch churches embrace the recovery movement. I still remember finding the first Christian national twelve-step organization, Overcomers Outreach. Later, many other churches, large and small, all over America, started various types of recovery meetings, which included lots of great recovery group names. Today Celebrate Recovery has made this movement more vogue and palatable to the mainstream church.

Christians today are seeing the wisdom of the recovery community. These groups were birthed in the 1930s with much prayer. At that time, no church would embrace them. Today, this child of the church has come back home with wisdom, grace, and the tools to help anyone and everyone willing to do the work to heal from whatever addiction plagues them.

I am a recovering person and have been writing recovery material for addiction for many years. I regularly see the miracle of recovery in my office in the Recovery Groups we've had for more than fifteen years.

Recovery for Everyone is not a new idea. The ideas in this book, the *Recovery for Everyone Workbook*, and *Recovery for Everyone Steps* have provided tried and true paths for sustained recovery and support that have worked very well with everyday people like you who lead groups.

You can be free! In the following pages, I am going to introduce you to some fundamental ideas that heal. The Lord Jesus died and rose from the dead so everyone can be free. As you do the work I detail here, you will see recovery and restoration in your life that can be amazing. In my decades of work in personal recovery, seeing men and women get free and stay free from their addictions and the consequences of living with an addict, I know you can have a life of recovery.

"Where the Spirit of The Lord is there is freedom."

2 Corinthians 3:17

Douglas Weiss, Ph.D.

#1
Time to Heal

I remember being in Bible college and crying out to God, fasting, praying, and begging to be set free, only to fall again and repeat the same plea week after week, month after month for all four years.

I had been radically saved. My alcohol and drug use fell off at that point and I've never had a desire for them since, but I couldn't get free from sexual addiction. I was learning about God and the Bible. I was part of a vibrant, passionate church that had great worship, where people got saved every week. I sang in the choir. I did evangelism. Nevertheless, my secret addiction held me in chains.

What's wrong with this picture? If you're an addict of any kind, you know exactly what I mean.

I want to assure you, your prayers and pleas have not gone unanswered, and that's why you're reading these pages today. Sadly, for me there was no addiction recovery in the church, no recovery workbook, no twelve-step programs...nothing. I had to learn recovery from the Lord and he taught me well.

I'll never forget it. After spending some time in recovery, I worked in a psychiatric hospital in the addiction unit. I was a seminary student at the time. Part of my job was to take alcohol and drug addicts to their addiction classes and twelve-step meetings. I spent years in smoke-filled rooms with people sober from alcohol and drugs, but not nicotine or coffee. Early on in that job, I decided to sit in on the addiction class. I threw my book bag down next to my chair. The counselor began facilitating a discussion on recovery with the patients, but I soon found myself attracted more to what was on the wall than the conversation the counselor was leading.

I found myself reading the Twelve Steps of Alcoholics Anonymous (see Appendix A). I thought back to the long road to healing Jesus had personally taken me through, to when I truly began to get free from my addiction. I probably looked distracted to my counselor because I was distracted! As I read through the steps I was able to clearly see how Jesus took me through each point of the steps and brought healing to my life.

This is not unusual with the way Jesus does things with me. Often, he asks me to obey him and then later exposes the scripture or principle he had me follow. In this chapter, I want to share with you some biblical principles so that you can see that recovery for everyone is greatly rooted in biblical truth. He is the author of our own freedom. He has given us all that we need to be free. We just need to know what these truths and principles are so we can go from struggling to recovery.

Before I go further on these principles, I want to share some powerful truths with you about who you are. You are a son or daughter of the Most High God. You are precious, wise, resourceful, and capable. You have a divine mission to break these curses off your life and clean up the damage from your past choices. God has chosen you to take the journey to recovery. Millions of people are saved, yet still addicted to many things, including relationships. Of all the people in pain who are crying out to God for help and freedom, God chose to give you the opportunity for recovery.

Recovery for Everyone is an opportunity. You decide what you do with this opportunity. You can push it away, do just a little to get out of a current crisis, or you can be consistent, do the work, become free, stay free for a lifetime, and be a part of seeing others get free and stay free as well.

Through Christ, God has already decided you are worthy of total freedom from every addiction. For me, that meant alcohol, drugs, sex, pornography, caffeine, and sugar. I know recovery, so I know that if you are ready, God wants you to be free! I just thought you should know that Father God thinks you're awesome and is very proud of you for taking this journey we call recovery.

Biblical Principle One: Confession

In Bible College, I cried out to God and constantly looked for scriptures to help me get free. Early in my walk with Jesus, I found a very familiar scripture that anyone who fails again and again can cling to for forgiveness. Here is what I found:

"If we confess our sins, he is faithful and just and will forgive us our sins and purify us from all unrighteousness" (1 John 1:9).

When I messed up, I did what you probably did as well. I knelt down, sometimes crying for Jesus to forgive and cleanse me. Like you, I experienced true forgiveness. I felt the forgiveness of Jesus. I believed his blood had more power than my sin in which I was choosing to participate. I felt cleansed and this would last for days or weeks until I acted out in the sin again; then wham-o! The guilt and shame came back and I would be forgiven again.

I think you get the picture. Most of you lived the same movie: act out in your addiction patterns (sin), ask for forgiveness, and do it all over again. This pattern is all too familiar for most of us.

I was confessing my sin to Jesus. He was forgiving me. Why wasn't I getting any better?

I had a client once say: "Yeah, I would ask Jesus to forgive me and then ask him to keep my behavior a secret and not tell my spouse, partner, friends, or anybody else. Imagine me asking Jesus, who is truth, to keep my secret." This was me, too, for years; confessing, wanting secrecy, and staying forgiven but not healed or free.

Why wasn't I getting free? Why wasn't God helping me? Why was I falling again and again? Well, quite simply, I was using the wrong principle to get the result I truly needed. Instead of just hanging out with I John, I needed another scripture that I'll share with you in a minute.

Remember how I said earlier that God often tells me to do something first (obey), then he shares with me the scripture or principle (revelation)? This was no different. So now I'll tell you the obedience part that preceded the revelation part.

As I told you, my desire for alcohol and drugs left me at my salvation commitment at nineteen years of age, though I first accepted Christ as a youth in a Salvation Army camp (thank God for the Salvation Army!). I struggled with my sexual addiction (mostly self-sex behavior). I was in seminary, working on my master's degree, preparing to go into full-time ministry.

I had a roommate in my dorm who was slightly different from me; a really awesome and gracious man of God. One day, I genuinely felt the Lord tell me to let my roommate know every time I participated in self-sex behavior. I was not excited about this at all, but my deal with God was to do 100 percent of what he told me to do, so I told my roommate what the Lord told me to do and he was okay with it.

Not even a week later, I needed the courage to tell my room-mate I had fallen. I never felt so humiliated in my entire life. He graciously forgave me. About a week or so later, I fell again and felt really humiliated when I told my roommate. However, some-thing wonderful happened after that second time. I genuinely did not want to do the behavior anymore. The desire to act waned greatly. I had a few more slips, but they were many weeks apart.

During the first few months of my recovery I committed to be totally honest if I slipped. The honesty led to me breaking the addiction for the first time in my life.

I have not participated in self-sex behavior or pornography in more than twenty-eight years. Occasionally, I even take a poly-graph to verify my recovery. I got free and stayed free, and God has used me to help others get free and stay free.

What made the difference? I started using the biblical principle in James 5:16:

"Therefore confess your sins to each other and pray for each oth-er so that you may be healed. The prayer of a righteous person is powerful and effective. "

"If" is really a critical part of this verse. This means "if" I confess, I can be healed or made free. If I don't confess, I am guaranteed to stay sick, or in my case, addicted. I was utilizing the principle of confessing my faults (acts or behavior) to another Christian of the same gender, so recovery and healing came to my life and stayed.

If you truly want to get free and stay free from your addiction behavior, be it alcohol, drugs, sex, codependency, work, car-bohydrates, sugar, nicotine, or caffeine, you HAVE TO con-fess to another person. To be free, you have to be honest and accountable to another person of the same gender. Let me tell you why in principle two.

Biblical Principle Two: Know Where the Healing Is

I'm going to get a little theological for a moment to explain where your healing and freedom is and why. I want to share with you a revelation that helped me make sense of why I needed to confess to another person to be made free. This is why "just Jesus and I" wasn't working, and why I couldn't get free earlier in my life.

After Jesus died on the cross and rose from the dead, he visited earth a few times. He was on the road to Damascus with two men, then with ten disciples, then with eleven disciples, and then with 500 of his followers (1 Corinthians 15).

Now, Jesus was with 500 people prior to the medicine era. Surely there was an opportunity to heal, but there's not one recording of the resurrected Christ doing any healing.

However, turn to the last page in the gospels and you'll find yourself in the book of Acts, and healing is happening everywhere (Acts 3:1-10). Amazing healing miracles happened through the apostles and other believers in Jesus. Why? The healing power of Jesus transferred from the head of Christ to the body of Christ. If you wanted healing or recovery, it was (and is) found inside other believers. I had been ignorantly going to the head of Jesus for what he places in his body. I was banging my head against the wall, thinking God didn't hear me or want to set me free. All along, I was simply going to the wrong place or using the wrong principle to get the results I truly needed, which was healing and recovery.

You see, like so many other Christians that have addictions, I was forgiven but I wanted healing or recovery. When I started to use the principle of confession, the healing and freedom in Christ's body was able to flow through my roommate to me. I was then able to get healed, get free, and stay free.

If you and I are 100 percent willing to get honest with another person of the same gender, we can heal and be free. If we protect our pride and our perceived spiritual reputation, we are guaranteed to stay sick. One of the major things I have learned in counseling people for more than twenty-five years is that "what you love is what you protect."

If you love your addictive choices and behavior, you will protect them. You will lie, minimize, blame, and get angry, sulk, or do whatever you have to do to not be 100 percent honest about your participation in your addictive choices or behavior. If you love real people in your life, including yourself, you will be 100 percent honest about your addictive choices and behaviors, protect the people you love, expose those choices and behavior to the light of another believer, and walk the path of recovery.

Biblical Principle Three: Understand Your Miracle May Be a Process

As an American or Western believer, culturally we are trained to appreciate the instantaneous in our lives, whether it be instant coffee, instant microwaveable food or popcorn, instant Internet access, instant cell phone access, and more. How many times a day do we push a button of some type and something occurs instantly?

When we come to Christ we sometimes carry this desire for immediate freedom. We see the many instantaneous, physical miracles in the Bible and wonder, "Why can't Jesus just touch me and get me free? Why do I have to do all of this recovery work to experience freedom? Why must I go through a process?"

Well, in the Bible there are both types of miracles: instantaneous and those that occur over time as a process. We see the instant healings of the blind being made able to see (Acts 9:17-18), the deaf being made able to hear (Acts 5:15), and even people being raised from the dead (Acts 20:7-10). However, the Bible also describes physical healings that occurred over time, particularly in Jesus' early ministry.

Recall the ten lepers Jesus told to go show themselves to the priest, and "as they went, they were healed" (Luke 17:11-15). They had to obey and put action into their obedience. As they obeyed, they were healed. Theirs was a process healing. Remember the man Jesus told to go wash in the pool of Bethesda. As the man bathed there, he was healed. In yet another example of obedience in action resulting in a process healing, recall the man Jesus told to stretch forth his withered hand. As he stretched it forth in obedience, he was healed.

Jesus decides if you'll experience an instant miracle or a process miracle, but both are true miracles. In the former, He does all the work, while in the latter, we have to participate for the miracle to occur. For me, freedom from alcohol and drugs were instant miracles. God took them away and I have never desired them since. Overcoming sex, pornography, caffeine, and sugar were process miracles for me. I used to ask why he had not just instantly delivered me from all of them. I have come to understand that process healing that leads to recovery from addiction has several added benefits over the instant miracle we might desire.

This recovery for everyone miracle gives you a humility that can last a lifetime: You know deep down you are a sinner and that you have been forgiven much. This process gives you genuine compassion and deeper love for others and yourself. This process allows you to give and receive from your brothers and sisters in Christ in an authentic manner. Process healing allows you to grow up spiritually, morally, and emotionally in the very areas where your addictive choices and behaviors stunted you. In many cases, this process gives you a ministry of healing and recovery you would likely not have had if you had been set free instantly.

God sometimes allows us to go through a miracle process because this way is actually better for us than an instantaneous healing might be. On this side of the process, going through it, learning it, teaching it, and duplicating it globally, I am grateful I was chosen for the process of the recovery miracle.

#2
Coming Home

There is a story about us addicts in the Bible. This story gives an outline of the addiction process as well as the principle for the road back. Our story of addiction is timeless, and so are the principles for recovery. Men and women have been medicating their pain and bad choices throughout time. God always desires for us to leave our addictions to follow him into spiritual adulthood. He is always willing to empower and enable us to do so when we are teachable and move from selfishness and making emotion-based choices to being other-focused and acknowledging our interconnectedness to others, firmly committed to a more principled way of living.

The famous story of the prodigal son offers the best illustration of this progression. If you have been a Christian for a while, it is likely you have heard this story preached or taught, but I would wager you have never heard it exactly the way God has opened it up to me over my many years of working with addicts and their spouses.

I am going to take this story apart piece by piece, but before I do, take a few minutes and read it in its entirety. I quote it here from Luke 15:11-32 (NIV):

11 Jesus continued: "There was a man who had two sons. 12 The younger one said to his father, 'Father, give me my share of the estate.' So he divided his property between them.

13 "Not long after that, the younger son got together all he had, set off for a distant country and there squandered his wealth in wild living. 14 After he had spent everything, there was a severe famine in that whole country, and he began to be in need. 15 So he went and hired himself out to a citizen of that country, who sent him to his fields to feed pigs. 16 He longed to fill his stomach with the pods that the pigs were eating, but no one gave him anything. 17 "When he came to his senses, he said, 'How many of my father's hired servants have food to spare, and here I am starving to death! 18 I will set out and go back to my father and say to him: Father, I have sinned against heaven and against you. 19 I am no longer worthy to be called your son; make me like one of your hired servants.' 20 So he got up and went to his father.

"But while he was still a long way off, his father saw him and was filled with compassion for him; he ran to his son, threw his arms around him and kissed him.

21 "The son said to him, 'Father, I have sinned against heaven and against you. I am no longer worthy to be called your son.'

22 "But the father said to his servants, 'Quick! Bring the best robe and put it on him. Put a ring on his finger and sandals on his feet. 23 Bring the fattened calf and kill it. Let's have a feast and celebrate. 24 For this son of mine was dead and is alive again; he was lost and is found.' So they began to celebrate.

25 "Meanwhile, the older son was in the field. When he came near the house, he heard music and dancing. 26 So he called one of the servants and asked him what was going on. 27 'Your brother has come,' he replied, 'and your father has killed the fattened calf because he has him back safe and sound.'

28 "The older brother became angry and refused to go in. So his father went out and pleaded with him. 29 But he answered his father, 'Look! All these years I've been slaving for you and never disobeyed your orders. Yet you never gave me even a young goat so I could celebrate with my friends. 30 But when this son of yours who has squandered your property with prostitutes comes home, you kill the fattened calf for him!'

31 "'My son,' the father said, 'you are always with me, and

everything I have is yours. 32 But we had to celebrate and be glad, because this brother of yours was dead and is alive again; he was lost and is found.'"

1. Entitlement

Luke 15:11-12: "Jesus continued: 'There was a man who had two sons. 12 The younger one said to his father, "Father, give me my share of the estate." So he divided his property between them.'"

Addicts of all kinds, whether addicted to exercise, sex, money, hoarding, chocolate, or anything else, live in what I like to call a "me" reality. They are all about them. Their self-absorption allows them to avoid simple principles or commandments like, "Honor your father and mother so that you may live long in the land the Lord your God is giving you" Exodus 10:12 (NIV).

The selfishness of addicts drives them to avoid all normal processes and relationships to get what they want. They want what they want and they want it now. They avoid principles like, "work for what you want." They would rather beg, borrow, steal, or manipulate people who care about them to get what they want.

As we get free from addiction, our poor choices, avoidance of basic principles, and manipulation of others who love us all stop. We move into taking responsibility for our present and past. If your past with an active addiction was all about you, you're not alone. Billions of us can relate to a period of time when we lived in a total "me" reality.

This prodigal son felt entitled to what his father had worked his whole life to acquire. The son relegated to his own selfish desires the fruit of decades of his father's hard work. The father became an object to the son, not a person or soul. To the son, his father was a means to an end, a thing to manipulate rather than a human being who loved him as a son.

In your addiction, write out some specific ways you felt entitled:

1._____

_____

2._____

_____

3._____

_____

4._____

_____

5._____

_____

6._____

_____

7._____

_____

8._____

_____

2. Immediacy

In an addiction, "right now" is an operating system. It's about me getting what I want, when I want, and I want it right now. Be it the codependent need to see their addicted friend, spouse, or child, the spending addict with their new toy, the gambler, or the carbohydrate or caffeine junkie, "right now" is the way they live life.

Driven by addiction, impatience keeps us from obtaining things through hard work, building relationships, or from having boundaries, and often leads us to illegal behavior. The now is the real way many of us lived. Whether we are junkies addicted to our cell phones, social media, news, or sports, the now is all-important. Immediacy of the now was our lifestyle in our active addiction state, and perhaps even into our early recovery.

Some of us approach recovery in a self-absorbed now state. We want our recovery now! We don't want to go to groups, have accountability, face consequences, read, pray, or love others. We resist engaging in recovery principles built into our lives which keeps us from developing the character these principles allow that would keep us free for a lifetime.

Give some examples of immediacy in your addiction:

1._____

_____

2._____

_____

3._____

_____

4._____

_____

5._____

_____

3. Alienation

Luke 15:13: "Not long after that, the younger son got together all he had, set off for a distant country..."

This young man got everything to which he thought himself entitled. It was not enough for him. He then did what so many addicts do, and alienated himself from his family and all those who truly loved him: friends, cousins, people in his spiritual community, and more.

Addiction makes you value "it" (whatever "it" is for you) more than people. They may not do so to the extreme the prodigal son did, taking his cash, belongings, some donkeys, and traveling hundreds or thousands of miles away from his father, but valuing "it" more than people is typical of the addict. Again, to them, people are objects to help them begin or maintain their addictive behavior. As a result, they will alienate themselves even from the people who truly love them the most: fathers or mothers, spouses, children, brothers or sisters, long-term friends, and more.

Remember, this was way back before a postal system, telephones, cell phones, email or any social media. This young man went totally off the grid from his father and everyone else, abruptly cutting off contact. In most cases, it starts off more gradually; less and less contact with family and friends, then not returning calls or emails, then maybe moving to another location so there is less chance of running into someone who might know you.

In your addiction, it is highly possible you will forsake all others for your addiction and even leave geographically.

List some of the people you alienated in your addiction and how you alienated them:

Name   How

1._____   1._____

2._____   2._____

3._____   3._____

4._____   4._____

5._____   5._____

6._____   6._____

4. No Accountability

When the disease of addiction starts to take over your thought processes and creates strongholds (beliefs you hold tight to that are in opposition to God's Word) one of the first strongholds is a perversion of the concept of recovery. The addict believes recovery is all about them doing what they want to do, when they want to do it, and not allowing anybody to tell them what to do. In AA they talk about this stronghold idea as "self-will run riot." It's all about me and I will not have any accountability for my behavior, be it drinking, drugs, sex, relationships, money, food, or any other.

The prodigal son moved himself real far away from home to ensure no one he had known would know where he was or what he was doing. He didn't want to deal with questions about who he was hanging around, how he was spending his money, or where he was all night.

Addicts in active addictions don't want to face challenging questions about their marriage or commitment to their addiction. Addictions of all types are emotion-based, so reason or reasonable questions about their choice to be in a relationship with their addiction confuse the addict. To avoid this confusion, they just avoid any accountability or honesty with people who might want to bring these to their lives.

Give examples of you avoiding accountability in your addiction.

1._____

_____

2._____

_____

3._____

_____

4._____

_____

5._____

_____

5. New People, Places, and Things

Luke 15:13: "...and there squandered his wealth in wild living."

I always say, "People who don't earn it don't know how to manage it," but this was worse. In verse thirty, the prodigal son's brother accuses him of spending his money on prostitutes (sex addiction). However, "wild living" may involve any number of things: alcohol, drugs, gambling, extravagant clothes, houses, spending/debt addiction, and more. Whatever it was, the prodigal son had received a lot of money—not just a few thousand dollars—and he had squandered it all. He could have started a business, married a woman, and had a life. Instead, he used people as things and became friends with like-minded people, and those relationships led him further and further into reinforcing a self-abounding lifestyle, regardless of his specific behavior.

Whatever your addictive behavior was, you too met new people like bartenders, drug dealers, other addicts, sex partners, and other people with a similar desire to engage in that behavior. While with them, you thought they cared, "got" you, or understood you best. You believed you could depend on them. You found that seemed true, as long as you were paying and giving yourself away to them in some manner.

The relationships you build while in an active addiction positively reinforce your behavior. You surround yourself with people who encourage you in your addictive behavior so you not only feel positive reinforcement for your drug or person of choice, but you create a dark cocoon that a sober mind would recognize as being wild, reckless, and thoughtless.

6. Depleted Resources

Luke 15:14: "After he had spent everything..."

Addictions, regardless of type, are leeches on human beings. This young man squandered all of his money. Imagine winning a huge amount of money through a lottery, then spending every last penny in a short amount of time. I don't know if his squandering was due to a spending addiction or simply the result of sex, alcohol, or another addiction. Regardless, every last penny was gone.

Addictions don't just rob you of money, they rob you of your ability to think rationally or express feelings maturely. They rob you of character, leaving you with a reputation for being quite foolish, so mature people don't and won't trust you.

Addictions rob you of spiritual resources, even causing a spiritual disconnect. Addictions rob you of emotional and moral development as well. This is why you can make the moral decision, "If I get caught, it's wrong," about lying, cheating, stealing, hating people, and more, rather than, "It's wrong because it's wrong," or "It's wrong because God says so."

The bad news is, your addiction depletes. The good news is, recovery reconnects you spiritually, emotionally, and morally. You can be restored to your original God-given design. Through our addictions, most of us have experienced depletion of some kind. As we gain our recovery we can experience a replenishing of our life like we never imagined.

List five ways you believe your addiction has depleted you in the past.

1._____

_____

2._____

_____

3._____

_____

4._____

_____

5._____

_____

7. Supernatural Circumstances

Luke 15:14: "...there was a severe famine in that whole country..."

God is God. He is much bigger than our little micro world. He is the God of the Nations. When he is moving you toward home, he can create all kinds of macro circumstances so that you experience need or pain. In most addiction stories, there is a story of a bizarre set of circumstances that resulted in some form of need or pain in the life of the addicted person.

Most of us have experienced some bizarre set of circumstances that led us to rethink our lives; a lost job, getting arrested, an illness, a car accident, a divorce, or getting caught in our addiction.

In the space below, list a few of the bizarre circumstances that caused you to rethink your life.

_____

_____

_____

_____

_____

8. Need

Luke 15:14: "...and he began to be in need."

This person with resources was living by what he hated to do. Now, after exhausting all his resources, he found himself in need. Need is a whole lot different from want. You may want a fancy blue coat, but when it's bitter cold, all you need is a coat—you're not picky. When you want steak rather than chicken, that's different from when you haven't eaten for days and you need food. The addicted may have many buddies to act out with, but they need a true friend. Need is different.

The need for health, for sanity, or to get your children or spouse back is a great motivation to reevaluate, rethink, and create a different life.

List the needs that came up for you as you drew close to the end of your addiction.

_____

_____

_____

_____

_____

_____

_____

9. First Attempt

Luke 15:15: "So he went and hired himself out to a citizen of that country, who sent him to his fields to feed pigs."

What strikes me as bizarrely interesting is that this prodigal's need didn't take him home. Bless our hearts, in our addiction states, addicts are highly independent and resourceful. Many of us make what I call "first attempts" to stop our addiction, or the impact from our addiction.

This young man went to the culture he was in to help him. He got a job. That might have helped a little bit to solve the eating problem, but not his heart problem.

Many addicts turn to their secular culture to help them with their addictions. Treating addictions is a mega business. Countless inpatient facilities and organizations attempt addiction treatment. Most of them are run by good people, and they do the best they know. Similarly, the man who hired the prodigal son was probably a good man, doing a good deed by helping a homeless person.

Since addicts so immerse themselves in secular ideas and people, this first attempt is honorable but incomplete. Good will not get us the freedom from addiction that Jesus Christ's death and resurrection can. Good won't give us the Holy Spirit to indwell us and help shape us into God's image. Good won't give us eternal life with the Father or an awareness of our divine purpose in time. These come when we come home.

However, to start on our journey toward recovery, most of us have attempted some version of self-help or cultured help.

In the spaces below, write out some of your first attempts at recovery.

_____

_____

_____

_____

_____

_____

_____

10. No one to Help

What's really interesting to me in this part of the story is something that is not portrayed. This young man had to have spent mega amounts of money over a period of many months on women, stores, bars, restaurants, giving to friends in need, and all the rest, to go through such a huge sum. He was probably thinking all these people were giving, like him. Day after day, no doubt he saw them making money. Yet when he plummeted to a place of genuine, dire need, how surprised he must have been when not one of his so-called friends was really there for him. Not one bartender, innkeeper, restaurant owner, friend, or brother even had a job to give to him.

He was alone the whole time in his addiction and was deceived that these people cared for him even a little bit. Addicts tend to surround themselves with other addicts so they're not confronted on their immature, selfish behavior. They are surrounded by other selfish, immature people who are in it for themselves and not real capable of genuine, caring relationships.

As an addict, you're not alone when you hit bottom. You were alone before that, but you created a fantasy world in which you fooled yourself about who the people around you actually were. When you're in real need, people who help you (like your group members) can become real friends to you.

List the names of a few people around you while your addiction was active that you thought of as real friends, only to later learn you were deceived about them and your relationship.

_____

_____

_____

_____

_____

_____

_____

_____

11. Trying Harder

Luke 15:16: "He longed to fill his stomach with the pods that the pigs were eating, but no one gave him anything."

When you go to the world to rid your spirit, soul, and body of attraction to addiction, things can get harder. Our prodigal thought, *I'll get a job, start solving my problems, get rid of my guilt, and utilize secular culture and godless solutions to get it done.*

It got worse. Though he had no job and was hungry before, now he was working all day in the heat and was still hungry. What he thought was a solution became another rip off. He was trying to fix an external problem but the disease of addiction, spiritual separation, and immaturity are internal problems solved by work and relationships.

Some of us have stories of trying harder before real recovery occurred in our lives. To try to stop our addictive behaviors and relationships, we went to doctors, counselors, and support groups, or turned to alternative medicine, New Age solutions, and good old self-will.

If this describes you, write down your fear of those experiences here.

_____

_____

_____

_____

_____

_____

_____

12. Waking Up

Luke 15:17: "When he came to his senses, he said, 'How many of my father's hired servants have food to spare, and here I am starving to death!"

This is a favorite verse for me. When it comes to recovery, coming to ourselves is the turning point to recovery for so many of us. The road is often hard and harder, but we do eventually hit what we call our bottom. At the end of us, we are out of resources, ideas, willfulness, and manipulation.

It is painful and freeing to realize we cannot do this and that what we are doing just plain doesn't work anymore. This is the power-less moment the Twelve Steps talk about. We come to the end of our life with our addiction. When you come to your senses, you start to see your addiction and your life differently, and with a little more clarity.

Describe the moment you came to your senses.

_____

_____

_____

_____

_____

_____

_____

_____

13. Having a Plan

Luke 15:18-19: "18 I will set out and go back to my father and say to him: Father, I have sinned against heaven and against you. 19 I am no longer worthy to be called your son; make me like one of your hired servants."

As a people group, addicts are very resourceful. You've heard some say they are "down but not out." Most addicts get totally depleted. Give them a moment and they get a second wind and hatch a plan.

The prodigal remembered what it was like to live under the blessings. No longer was he full of entitlement, arrogance, and self-will. He was ready to submit to authority, follow the rules of his father, and serve instead of being served.

Due to a huge heart transformation, the prodigal son becomes broken of self-will, ceases living for self, and is then willing to do the business at hand. His plan came complete with what he had to do and needed to say.

Some of you reading this may be struggling with self-will. You don't want to submit to a person or a process, even if these could free you from your current addiction. Overvaluing your opinions and will can make your road to healing longer and more painful for both you and those who love you.

Surrendering is crucial to success. I had to do what I was told in order to heal. To get free, I had to submit to others, follow some principles, and be willing to serve. Whether you are coming home to the Father's house for the first time or one of several, It is time to decide to return and submit to him.

The prodigal son felt unworthy. You may feel this way as well. Know this: Jesus' blood makes you worthy. If you have never said the following prayer, I recommend you stop reading, say it out loud, and return home to the Father: "Jesus, come into my heart and forgive me of my sins. I accept you as Lord of my life, and I will follow you."

When did you start creating a plan to give up your addiction that involved submission, principles, and service? What did that first plan look like?

_____

_____

_____

_____

_____

_____

_____

14. Change of Direction

Luke 15:20: "So he got up and went to his father."

This is the turning point of the whole story. Without this one verse, this man's story would have been just another fantasy to be free. However, this small verse is packed with important ideas that are necessary for those of us who want recovery to truly get it.

Here is an important question: Where was this man when he destroyed his own life? That's right; he was still in a distant country.

He was probably hundreds or thousands of miles from home.

This was not a two-day walk; it required weeks, perhaps months. He had to walk constantly and persistently in the opposite direction of his addiction lifestyle. He had to forsake people, places, and things he might have grown fond of in his addiction. He had to leave all with which he had become familiar and walk a long way to reach home.

Some people preach this scripture as if the son repented and his father jumped into the pigpen and hugged him. That's just not true at all. The father was at home. The son had to do all the work, day after day. The son had to deny the impulse to be lazy, organize his resources to walk again, and implement his recovery plan.

Like him, you are going to have to do life differently to get recovery. You may need to give up people, places, and things to which you are emotionally attracted. You're going to have to make time to do recovery work: complete the workbooks, attend the meetings, make phone calls, and face the real issues. You're going to have to consistently, persistently stay focused on the Father and walk a different walk...every day.

Recovery can be measured. If you're doing the work, you want to be free. If you're not doing the work, you only wish to be free, but are unwilling to do what recovery requires.

The son had done the work of recovery daily, consistently, over a long period of time. Every day his character improved. No alcohol, no prostitutes, no crazy spending, no out of control behavior; he made a complete change in his life's direction. Broken of self-will, determined to be free from his past, committed to serve others, he found his recovery.

15. Restoration

Luke 15:20-24: 20 "But while he was still a long way off, his father saw him and was filled with compassion for him; he ran to his son, threw his arms around him and kissed him.
21 "The son said to him, 'Father, I have sinned against heaven and against you. I am no longer worthy to be called your son.'
22 "But the father said to his servants, 'Quick! Bring the best robe and put it on him. Put a ring on his finger and sandals on his feet.
23 Bring the fattened calf and kill it. Let's have a feast and celebrate. 24 For this son of mine was dead and is alive again; he was lost and is found.' So they began to celebrate."

This is the part of the story everyone loves. After the son changed his behavior constantly and persistently over time, he was changed inside and out. The boy who left was perfumed, arrogant, and entitled. The son who came back was broken, dirty, humble, repentant, and willing to be of service.

When the father saw his son approaching, he ran down the driveway, hugged and kissed him, and welcomed him home. The father clothed and restored him as a son (not a slave) and celebrated the relationship.

God wants every addict who takes the journey and does the hard work of recovery to be fully restored as a son or daughter of the Most High God and be rid of all slavery thinking and behaving. His desire is to see them restored to him and to family members and friends.

You are on an amazing journey. Some of you feel (rightly so) that you're on the walking back stage of this story. I say...keep walking. Some of you are in the restoring aspect of this story, changing your stinking slavering thinking to that of a child of God; one He loves deeply. He wants you home and playing your part in the Father's business.

Your recovery is 100 percent your responsibility. You will need to work hard, make the calls, submit to the principles, and do life differently than you did when you were doing only what you wanted to do.

I know from personal experience the work and journey are worth it. You have no idea how amazing your life can be and how you can become an important part of the miracle of recovery in other people's life.

#3
Am I Addicted?

I know better than most that Christians often have some difficulty with the word or concept of addiction (at least part of our Christian family does). If you are reading this book, it is likely you accept the concept of addiction and you or someone you care about is struggling with out of control behavior. You may well be asking, *What makes such behaviors an addiction?*

In the following pages we are going to take a look at the qualifiers for addiction. These qualifiers apply whether you were a workaholic, shopaholic, alcoholic or intimacy anorexic. Read each addiction qualifier with an open mind and see if any (or several) of them apply to your out of control behavior process or that of someone else in your life.

1. Efforts to Stop

In this qualifier, the addict has come to a place, whether internally or externally, where they get motivated, apply effort, or to try and stop an addictive behavior. This is a moment of clarity for the addict when they realize that what they are doing isn't working anymore, and they begin to make some effort to stop the addictive behavior.

These rational moments can be due to an internal crisis from the pain they are in or a realization of the pain they are creating for themselves. More often, these low moments are externally stimulated by those around them. Perhaps the addict loses a job, a lover, a spouse, or has some legal or financial problem due to his or her addictive behavior, and momentarily attempts to stop the behavior.

Most addicts struggle with some internal pain that provokes them to think they should change. Sometimes they follow through with an attempt to limit or control the addictive issue in their life. Usually, however, these efforts eventually fail. The external pain addicts experience at the failure often causes them to relapse. They must replace efforts to limit or control addictive behavior and with the work required to gain recovery from addiction.

I have made attempts to stop my addictive behavior.

Y_____   N_____

2. "Read My Lips"

This was part of a classic quote from George H.W. Bush during his first presidential campaign. He looked straight into the TV camera and made a promise not to raise taxes, beginning with, "Read my lips." As time passed and circumstances changed, he did exactly what he promised not to do, raised taxes, thus negating his promise and turning "read my lips" into the epitaph for his re-election hopes.

In politics, we expect broken promises; that seems to be the norm. Similarly, in addiction, not keeping promises is also a norm. Addicts promise their parents, probation officer, boss, lover, sibling—just about anybody—that they are going to stop their addiction, whatever it is. Sometimes these promises are just internal. After something painful or humiliating has occurred, they say to themselves, "I need to stop." Sometimes in the morning they just look into the mirror, straight into their own eyes and say, "That's the last time. I am never doing that again." They make promises to themselves and others and just don't keep them.

Their addictive behavior continues for days, weeks, months, or years. There is a promise made, sometimes sincere, to stop a behavior; however, the promise is void because the addictive behavior repeats.

I have made promises and broken them as it relates to my addictive behaviors.

Y_____   N_____

3. Consequences

Every addiction has consequences. The consequences can be a smashed car, broken relationships, or a damaged reputation. All types of things can happen as addicts tighten their grip on their addiction and lose their grip on reality.

Your consequences will be unique to your addiction. The food addict might have issues with weight, or back and knee pain. The exercise addict might experience bodily injury. The alcohol or drug addict might suffer legal issues or financial problems. The shopping or gambling addict might incur staggering debt. If you're addicted, it is likely you have suffered or are still suffering the consequences of your chosen addictive behaviors.

I have suffered the consequences of my chosen addictive behaviors.

Y_____   N_____

4. Keeping it Going

In the movie, *Planes, Trains and Automobiles,* starring Steve Martin and John Candy, two guys travel across America trying to arrive at a certain destination in time for Thanksgiving. Yet at every turn it seems terrible things would happen to them (consequences). Regardless of their consequences, they were determined to keep going. Even when it became extremely difficult (and ridiculous), they kept going to fulfill their commitment.

This is a great picture of addicts of any kind. They are committed to their addiction. They incur loss after loss, consequence after consequence, but instead of getting sober to what is happening, they get more committed to the addiction and keeping it going. They continue to use their "drug," regardless of the consequences.

When someone is rational, they learn from consequences. When someone is truly addicted, it is as if the part of the brain that learns hits a pause button. Even after suffering consequences (even significant consequences) of their addictive behaviors involving a substance, process, or person, they return to these behaviors again and again.

If you're in a relationship with an addict, whether he or she is a friend or family member, this is when you will think they are crazy. You say something like this: "How could you go back to that after x, y, or z has just happened to you?"

Using your addictive chemical, process, or person after suffering consequences is one definite distinction between having a problem and having an addiction. Keep reading, however; there is more to help you separate these two realities.

I have used my chemical, process or person after having consequences.

Y_____   N_____

5. Do More, Do More

In addiction, there is a place where you get obsessed. This is found in the addict who does more and more. The cocaine addict may empty her savings to use more and more. The spending addict gets another credit card even when he can't pay the last three credit cards he has.

"More" looks different for everyone: more caffeine, more work, more helping others, more drinking, more using, more sex, more Internet, more cell phone usage, and so on. More is just more. What was an hour a week on Facebook becomes three hours a day. One drink becomes a bottle. One romantic relationship becomes several people online you're "just talking to."

The "do more" obsession is much more obvious to those around addicts than to the addicts themselves. Denial about engaging more in the addictive substance, process, or person is very common when someone is active in his or her addiction. As they get sober or free, addicts become much more aware of their "do more" obsession with the addictive behavior in their lives.

I have experienced the "do more" obsession with my addictive behavior.

Y_____   N_____

6. Takes More

In the field of addiction we use the term "tolerance." Tolerance is simply when one builds up a resistance to an addictive behavior and has to do more of the behavior to get a desired result. Tolerance can also mean one doesn't get as much out of the behavior as one once did. Either way, tolerance is frustrating to the addict. While at first, it took a beer for the alcoholic to feel better, it now takes whiskey—and that might not even be satisfying. While a shopaholic used to get a rush from spending $50, it now takes $500 and still doesn't quite scratch the itch. The workaholic who started at seventy hours a week now feels the need to work more. Tolerance is real...and it's really frustrating.

Your tolerance will be unique to your addictive issue. In their addiction, most addicts have experienced a tolerance or "this isn't doing it for me anymore" type of feeling. If experienced consistently, the addict begins to up the ante (so to speak), to either do more, do differently, or do both to recreate that escape reality high that they once experienced at lower levels or frequency of this behavior.

I have had a tolerance experience in my addiction.

Y_____   N_____

7. More Time

All addictions take time. Those who gamble increase their time as the addiction grows. Those who use drugs, alcohol, food, or sex also utilize more time as the addiction grows. The same applies to hoarding. An anorexic will spend more time obsessing about what he or she is not going to eat that day.

It makes sense: If you have tolerance and you "logically" assume you need to do more and more, your more and more will take significantly more of your time. Again, the addicts themselves don't feel their time slipping away. Their late night, early mornings, or taking "some time off of work" makes sense to them because the addiction is requiring more of them to grow stronger.

Addicts might feel they are really living and really free by spending more time with their addiction. However, the exact opposite is actually true. The more time we give to the addiction the stronger the addiction, and the attributes of addiction grow deeper in our hearts and minds.

I have spent more time over the course of an addictive behavior.

Y_____   N_____

8. The Blues

Every addiction has a dark side. Even those who use drugs that go up have stories of the coming down. The shopper has the high in the mall, but regret when the credit card bill comes. The sex addict gets exhilaration in his or her behavior, but also experiences the downside of the shame. As the soul increases its dependence on addiction to medicate or deal with life, it is very common to have withdrawals from the drug when it is not available. Those with chemical addictions may also suffer physical symptoms: sweats, unusual temperatures, aches, headaches, disorientation, and more.

Try this with a cell phone addict: Take their phone away. Do this to even the sweetest Christian woman and she can become as hostile as a grizzly defending her cub. Even worse: Take a cell phone addict to a place that has no cell service for multiple days. You'll see the various stages of anger, sadness...and even some twitching going on.

All this may sound funny, but only because most of us know a cell phone addict. They touch their phones before they touch their spouses! The blue side or withdrawals are true for most addictive substances, processes, and even people. Having some psychological withdrawal from process or people addictions is actually quite common. You'll see a love addict or codependent go through withdrawal when they can't get access to the person they love.

I have had some form of withdrawal when getting off of my addictive behavior.

Y_____   N_____

9. Decreasing Other Activities

As the addiction cries out for more and more, like a starving animal requiring more and more food, or a lover requiring more and more time, how does the addict respond? All of us have only twenty-four hours in a day and can only be one place at a time, so we have to start making decisions, including addicts.

The crux of the decision for the addict is, "Do I give to more to reality, responsibilities, and real relationships, or do I give more to the addiction?" Addicts give more to the addiction. This means decreasing time with their work, family, friends, church, sporting activities, and even entertainment.

Additionally, as you deplete your energy in your addiction, you are actually less present in any real activities you are lassoed into. You actually decrease how much you are genuinely engaged when you are physically with friends or family. The only addiction process this isn't true for is intimacy anorexia. These addicts are trying to create distance with their spouse, so they engage in more and more activities outside of the home to feed their addiction process.

I give more to my addiction that I do to reality, responsibilities, and real relationships.

Y_____   N_____

10. My Score

Whether we like it or not, part of education is the proverbial pop quiz. Well, here we go to do our pop quiz on our addiction behaviors. In the space below, put all your yes and no answers beside each heading:

Efforts to Stop   Takes More

Y_____   N_____   Y_____   N_____

"Read My Lips"   More Time

Y_____   N_____   Y_____   N_____

Consequences   The Blues

Y_____   N_____   Y_____   N_____

Keep it Going (after consequence)   Decreasing Other Activities

Y_____   N_____   Y_____   N_____

Do More, Do More

Y_____   N_____

Now, what I have shared with you are classic symptoms of addiction. These same symptoms are those a counselor or doctor would use to assess if someone has an addiction (though they use clinical terms for them). It's similar to a doctor assessing whether you have a cold, strep throat, depression, or hypothyroidism. They run your symptoms through a grid which points them to the specific diagnosis. Whether a person is saved or not does not change the diagnosis.

Now, say a man goes to the doctor. He fits the full criteria for whatever illness or disorder the doctor is assessing. Imagine this conversation:

"You have X diagnosis," the doctor says.

The man responds politely, "I can't have diagnosis X; I'm saved." This may sound silly, but there are people who fully fit the addiction symptoms, but deny they are addicted because they are saved. (If you've gotten this far into this book, you probably don't have this issue.)

Now I'll reveal the answer to our pop quiz. If you responded "yes" more than three times, it is likely you have an addiction issue in your life. Check one of the boxes below:

☐ I have an addiction issue.

☐ I do not have an addiction issue.

If you have an addiction issue, please write out the chemical, pro-cess, or person related to your addictive behavior in the space below! If you write more than one, draw a star beside the one you are currently addressing.

_____

_____

_____

_____

_____

_____

_____

#4
Psychological Aspects and the Six Types

For some addicts, soul aspects have a great bearing on their addiction. Let's take a moment and discuss the soul. The soul is the mind, will, and emotions. Many addicts, regardless of the addiction type, have to heal the soul realm to get and stay free. Not all addicts have soul issues, but most do. Many addicts who have sought treatment report that they have come from abusive backgrounds, including physical, sexual, and spiritual abuse or neglect. In this chapter, we will focus on these abuses and neglect, and then discuss the different types of addicts.

Abandonment

Abandonment is experienced primarily in the family of origin, though not exclusively. I believe it is God's plan that children be cared for and nurtured within the family unit. Yet in our culture, abandonment issues are greater than they have ever been, even in Christian families. This is especially evident in the twenty-first century because of increasingly high divorce rates.

Personally, I have never met my biological father. My legal father and mother divorced when I was young, and I grew up in many foster homes. Losing a primary figure in life due to death or divorce can be unimaginably painful and confusing for a child. The need to have both parents engaged in a child's life throughout the childhood years is very strongly supported in research literature. When the child's need for two parents goes unmet, as the child grows, the consequences and emotional pain can set him or her up to turn to some form of addictive behavior to medicate the pain in his or her soul. The medicine a soul chooses may depend on what is available or the role modeling of medication use behavior in the home.

The souls of many children and teenagers have been deeply wounded due to abuse or neglect. The pain of abuse or neglect can set you up to want to medicate. For example, when you have a toothache, you desire to ease the pain. When your soul is in pain from abuse or neglect, it wants to ease the pain through addictive behavior or relationships.

Now I will expound on the forms of abuse or neglect you may have suffered during your development years.

Abuse

Abuse is commonly reported by addicts as the root of their addiction. Here are just a few kinds of abuse children might experience in their early development years.

Physical abuse—Being slapped in the face or being hit excessively and/or inappropriately with or without explanation is a form of physical abuse. Some people have grown up with a parent who had an addiction and were physically abused by the parent when the parent was in the midst of his or her addiction. Flashbacks of being physically hurt, abused, and violated makes a child question his safety. Children who have lived in these circumstances will commonly question their self-worth because a primary caregiver violated and abused them instead of providing a caring relationship.

Emotional abuse—Kids often experience emotional abuse in the form of shaming by a primary caregiver. They also experience emotional abuse when a primary caregiver makes them overly responsible for their behavior. Assigning children to inappropriate age development tasks is another form of emotional abuse. All of these behaviors cause pain for developing children and bring dysfunction to their family system. Emotional abuse can predispose children to choose a form of addiction to act out in order to medicate the pain.

Spiritual abuse—Spiritual abuse occurs when spirituality is used as a mood-altering state as opposed to a living relationship with God. There appears to be a great difference in people who approach God relationally compared with those who approach him as an object. Some addicts have grown up in families that forced them into a belief system and shamed them for questioning the system. They were unable to explore spirituality or even Christianity for themselves. Consequently, they were shamed with religious language for having any beliefs that differed from their parents.

Sexual abuse—This form of abuse can overwhelm the spirit, soul, and body of a human being. It is an abuse that violates the inner core of who a person is. Research shows that sexual abuse can set one up for sexual preoccupation (such as an early fantasy life), to act out sexually, or to completely shut down sexually. The list of the effects of sexual abuse goes on and on.

Children have very few skills to be able to process or deal with sexual abuse. This abuse forces a child into an adult world he or she is not ready for cognitively, in either feelings or choices. When the reality of the abuse comes to light, it is very painful. Often, victims of sexual abuse do not remember the abuse until after they are well into their recovery, when memories they have suppressed even since early childhood suddenly begin to surface.

People of either gender can perpetrate sexual abuse on an addict. This is worth emphasizing, due to the common cultural misconception that sex between an older female and a younger male (for example, a twelve-year-old boy and a sixteen-year-old girl) is not sexual abuse. Some even hold the view that this as a positive experience. This is simply not true.

One sex addict who came to my office told me that when he was thirteen years old, he went to his friend's house to play. His friend wasn't there but the boy's mother was, and she invited him in and engaged in sexual behavior with him. This behavior continued until the day before his wedding, at age thirty. He could not allow himself to believe that this experience with his friend's mother was sexual abuse. He was referred to me because he was suffering from major depression. When I counseled him, he was having seven affairs at one time and couldn't handle it. It was clear there was a direct link for him between his childhood abuse and addiction, regardless of the gender of the abuser.

Sexual abuse pushes the victim into experiencing sex as a sexual object—to objectify sexuality. This experience creates a need to medicate to escape the pain. Sexual addiction can be one of those medications.

Sexual abuse can affect the addict not only in choosing an addiction to medicate the pain, but also in choosing or avoiding specific sexual behaviors due to the confusion the abuse caused.

Neglect

Our culture is finally recognizing that neglect is just as damaging as the forms of trauma and abandonment we have already covered. Neglect is defined as a parent's irresponsibility toward his or her child's development in any area.

Spiritual neglect—Spiritual neglect is an absence of spiritual information and development. A spiritually neglected child is typically not encouraged to connect with God. Even discussion about God may be totally absent from the home. This can leave a child feeling incomplete. Spiritual neglect can cause a child to feel unaccountable to God.

Physical neglect—When a child's physical needs are not met, it can set him or her up for pain that will eventually require medication. Forms of physical neglect can include: a child being humiliated by others because he or she does not have appropriate attire for school; a child not being given enough food to eat or adequate nutrition; a child being physically abandoned by his or her parents for several days at a time, or; a child being deprived of necessary medical treatment. These forms of physical neglect can be just as traumatizing as some forms of physical abuse. In some cases, both neglect and abuse occur at the same time. The combination of neglect and abuse only compound the pain many addicts experienced while growing up.

Emotional neglect—The following is a metaphor that is useful in understanding what emotional neglect can do, especially in one's early development.

I believe the human being has a sponge inside that needs water on a regular basis. This sponge is their individuality, personhood, and the way they see themselves. The water the sponge needs is approval, praise, encouragement, and affirmation. Many who have grown up in dysfunctional families can quickly conclude that their sponge was never watered. They have a sense of emotional deprivation. Their sponge just got drier and drier because they didn't know how to ask for their needs to be met. They were not the adult in the situation. Now, as an adult, there is an internal ache in their inner being, and it stems from emotional neglect. One or both parents may have been distant or emotionally absent. Recovery can actually be the very first experience they have in receiving praise and affirmation from someone. Everyone needs to hear praise, affirmation, and encouragement—and we don't need to be ashamed of this need.

If you were emotionally neglected, as you move along in your recovery, you will realize that you don't need to be ashamed that you need to receive emotional support and encouragement. The dryness inside that needs to be medicated in your addiction was set up early in life. Addiction provided a place for emotional nurturance through creating a world of fantasy—a world that is nurturing and encouraging. This often was the safest place to go, a place where you could escape the emotional absence in your home environment and gain some kind of emotional support, even though it was a false place. Giving up addiction is not only about giving up inappropriate behavior or relationships. It is often about giving up the first caring relationship the addict may have experienced, whether it was a relationship with a bottle, drugs, unhealthy people, or working. This false relationship has been primary and is what has helped the addict get through life. In light of all this information, it is easy to see how addiction often replaces the emotional neglect a person suffered.

Sexual Neglect—American literature has little to say about sexual neglect, even though it is a very common phenomenon. Many of us have experienced growing up in a family where we received little or no sexual information from our parents. Research shows that most sexual information adults receive when they were children came from peers who knew just as little about sex as they did.

Sexual neglect is typically a result of the old rule where "we don't talk about sex," even though most are experiencing it. Sexual neglect can breed confusion and unnatural inquiry while one tries to identify and relate to an expression of our own sexuality.

Memorably, one addict said he grew up in a home where sex was considered a dirty, bad thing, yet one was to save it for the one you love. This was the message he received in his Christian home. It is quite an ironic message: You give the most disgusting gift you can to the person you love most! This is a message that many of us received in our growing up years.

Others reported learning from other sources. Some have said they received pornography as their sexual education from one of their parents. The bottom line in these situations is, someone who is deprived of sexual information has only their own childlike investigative procedures to solve their internal development problems. As a holistic approach to addiction, I believe the psychological aspects of addiction are very important for each addict to consider and investigate during their recovery journey.

Sexual neglect can set the addict up to medicate the absence of accurate information about sex explained by a primary caregiver during their development. As we explore these forms of neglect and abuse, you will see that each one can set up a cavity in the soul of the addict that needs filling, explaining, and interacting. If this pain goes untreated, over time it will become more intense and will drive the addict to find solace somewhere. Some find solace in alcohol, drugs, or sex. Neglect or abuse issues can be the primary cause of addiction for some, but a secondary cause for others.

The Six Types of Addicts

It's been more than twenty-five years now since I treated my first addicted client. In the earlier years many paradigms of understanding and treating addicts were the best guess at the time.

As a field, addiction has grown considerably. As a clinician and now a psychologist, I have looked into the souls of many addicts and discovered that not all addicts are alike. Intuitively, when an addict attends a support group they also realize they are not alike as well.

I often share a paradigm with my clients they find to be very helpful. I begin by covering the six types of addicts briefly. Before I expound on the six types, let me go back to a verse that really helped me understand humans and addictions and why they are different for different people. In 1 Thessalonians 5:23, Paul says we are to sanctify our spirit, soul, and body:

"May God himself, the God of peace sanctify you through and through. May your whole spirit, soul and body be kept blameless at the coming of our Lord Jesus Christ."

What I understand of this scripture is that strengths and weaknesses can be found in spiritual areas of our lives, our soul realm (mind, will and emotions), or in our bodies. The body piece gets quite a lot of attention in neuroscience, specifically regarding hormones, nutrition, and general chemical balances in our bodies and brains. Working with addicts day after day for years, I realized that not only was the origin of their addiction important, but that understanding the origin is important as well and affects what their treatment will need to be.

I will now briefly describe the six types of addicts. My hope is that you will see how this information can help you to heal and be free for the rest of your life.

Addictions can involve both substances (alcohol, drugs, sugar, carbohydrates, caffeine, and others) and processes (gambling, relationships, love, work, sex, and more). In these short descriptions, I will not be able fully detail your particular addiction. That's one of the limitations of writing a general addiction book. If you find the biological aspects of addiction interesting, there are many books that focus on specific addictions that you may find helpful

The condition of the body is a key factor in one becoming addicted to a substance or process. The first kind of addict starts life chemically or hormonally challenged, which causes discomfort, imbalance, or depression. This person will definitely look for a biological solution for his or her nagging problem. The first time this person ingests alcohol or drugs, or engages in a process that causes the chemicals to rise that they need to compensate for the deficit in their bodies, and they feel whole or great. They repeat ingesting the substance or engaging in the process to continue getting that elated feeling. That is, until they become addicted. In this case, the "medicine" (addiction) for the body's imbalance becomes the problem.

The second kind of addict from a biological aspect has a relatively healthy body, but through repetition creates a dependence on a substance or process to feel a certain way. In some cases, like sex and substances, the neuropathic highways of the brain can be hijacked. When this happens, one's body becomes the enemy, demanding the candy (addiction) that you have been reinforcing to feel the mood state it creates, whether a substance or process.

The body part of "spirit, soul and body" has been largely overlooked in Christian recovery models. Christians like to just focus on only the spiritual. However, Paul encourages us to look at the whole person. This approach to healing and obtaining recovery makes more sense to me than focusing on only one dimension of our three-dimensional being.

You need only see someone go through withdrawal, whether from drugs, alcohol, sex, relationships, or work, to realize that the body aspect is real. Addicts have withdrawals that are partially physical, such as convulsions, sweats, and shakes. This is important to understand, particularly if physical aspects are part of your addiction process. Also, if you are a person who grew up in a healthy family with no trauma or abuse, it is important to know you might have become addicted purely due to biological reinforcement.

Psychological Addict

Research related to addiction has found that generally, a larger population of addicts has suffered some form of abuse or neglect. These people find the combination of messages in the fantasy world and the chemical cocktail to the brain to be a salve unto their hurting souls. Simply put, they medicate the past or the pain in their souls by acting out, which is their form of medicine.

In my clinical experience, eighty percent of addicts (or more) have abandonment, abuse, or neglect issues of some type in their past. These painful events will ultimately need to be addressed for the addict to fully heal. Some of these issues are addressed in the *Recovery for Everyone Workbook*.

The Spiritual-Based Addict

This addict is looking for a spiritual connection in all the wrong places. In recovery, we talk about our spiritual hole. Such addicts put their addiction (whether chemical or process) in a hole but find it doesn't scratch the itch over time. Should they have a spiritual awakening of some type, their addictive behaviors cease because they have filled their spiritual hole. They then pursue life in a healthy manner.

These are the people who accept Jesus Christ as Lord and Savior and their addictions stop instantly. This is what happened to me and my addictions to alcohol and drugs. My addictions left when I became a Christian, though my sex addiction stayed and I needed to heal from that.

I tell my Christian clients, "If he didn't deliver you, he wants to heal you through the recovery process. Either way is a miracle!"

The Trauma-Based Addict

The trauma-based addict has experienced sexual trauma as a child or adolescent. This trauma becomes the major pain they are medicating. For some addicts, this is their biggest secret. They suppress the pain. However, this pain must be addressed and healed.

If you have suffered the trauma of sexual abuse or rape, you absolutely must tell someone so that you can begin to heal. This secret lodged in your spirit, soul, and body needs to be exposed to be healed. I was abused in my early years. It wasn't my fault. Victims of sexual abuse often take false responsibility for the abuse and this must be worked through. If you were abused or raped, it was not your fault: You were not responsible for it.

The trauma-based addict has to address the abuse they suffered to stop the acting out, be it substance or process addiction behaviors. Find a pastor, recovery person, or counselor of the same gender with whom you can be honest.

This category of trauma includes those who have experienced abortions. Women especially suppress this trauma, so their secret can be the core of the pain they are medicating. When men who willingly participated in an abortion hold onto their secret, it often becomes a big factor in their addiction behaviors. If this is your trauma, again, speak to someone of the same gender and start to expose your secret.

For the trauma-based addict, the trauma determines the flavor of the addiction. This trauma must be addressed for the addict to heal.

The Intimacy Anorexic Addict

Intimacy anorexia is an addiction process all by itself. However, from my experience working with addicts of various kinds, this addiction cannot only coexist with, but exacerbate a chemical or process addiction in one's life.

Look at the list of intimacy anorexia characteristics below. Which of these would your spouse or partner say apply to you? If you believe five or more of these apply to you, you are probably an intimacy anorexic.

1. Withhold love from your spouse
2. Withhold praise or appreciation from your spouse
3. Control your spouse by way of silence/anger
4. Criticize your spouse without grounds, regularly
5. Withhold sex
6. Blame spouse for everything
7. Stay very busy to avoid your spouse
8. Control/Shame with money issues
9. Unable to share feelings with your spouse
10. Withhold spiritual connection from your spouse

Many addicts who try to get sober but keep having what I call "flat tire" recovery (relapse regularly) meet the criteria for intimacy anorexia. If you have been sober from addictive acting out behaviors for a year, but your spouse wants to leave you because "nothing's changed," you too might be an intimacy anorexic.

The Addict With Mood Disorders

Some adolescent or young adult addicts have chemical imbalances. These young people find the addictive chemical or process offers them a way to medicate or alter their chemical imbalance. They use this medicating response quite regularly, and over time, create an addiction. In a journal article I wrote called, "The

Prevalence of Depression in Male Sex Addicts Residing in the United States," I discovered that 28 percent of male sex addicts suffered from depression.

A second common chemical imbalance I see in my practice with addicts is cyclothymic disorder. This is a slight up-and-down fluctuation in mood addicts usually experience on roughly a weekly basis (a funky day). This type of addict will need to do all the recovery work discussed here and in the exercise workbook. In addition, he or she should see a psychiatrist for medication for the mood disorder.

Can I Be More than One Type?

Absolutely! Most addicts overlap into more than one of the types just briefly described. Once you know the type of addict you are, you can follow a treatment plan for your type that can be very beneficial for you.

When you begin your recovery, you really need to be fully informed. Continue to read the solution aspects of this book.

Remember, your recovery affects many people in your life. I have been sober for more than twenty-seven years, without a relapse. Not only has my life been positively affected, but so have the lives of everyone close to me. You deserve enduring recovery for your life as well! Everyone deserves recovery! Today is the day to begin your recovery.

#5

The "New" Addiction Cycle

A New Perspective

Over the past twenty-five years of treating addiction I have noticed specific patterns appearing among addicts in my practice as they move from normal life toward the zone of the addiction. Several clinicians in the area of addiction are trying to define this trip the addict takes.

The question we are grappling with is how a perfectly sane person can repetitively choose addiction behaviors against their better judgment, especially when they are saved. Personally and professionally, I know that there is a quantum leap between reality and addiction. In the next few pages I will discuss a path many of us have traveled from sanity to insanity. I call this map to insanity the New Addiction Cycle.

We will first explore the four broad aspects of four pain agents: emotional discomfort, unresolved conflict, stress, and a need to connect. You can discover which of these four primary pain agents relates to you and your life, while determining if any of the others apply to you. These pain agents and others move the addict toward the next level of the addiction cycle.

Before I go into the addiction cycle, there is an important spiritual dynamic to mention that occurs as we move from normal to insanity. Somewhere along the way in the addiction cycle, we no longer fear or honor God. The timing of our disconnection from God can differ from person to person, and even per occurrence. However, early on, this can be very challenging in our recovery. Honoring God is something we grow into as we begin to get freedom. Spiritual maturity is a part of what recovery gives back to us, and that is honoring God.

I. Pain Agents

Most addicts, as we have discussed in previous chapters, have experienced biological, soul, and/or spiritual reasons for their addiction. What I have experienced in working with addicts is that they typically have a need to escape and not feel the pain they have experienced in the past. Many addicts have developed a coping mechanism to escape from the pain of a childhood and/or adolescent trauma. This coping mechanism for escape has carried the addict through most of his or her adult life. When things get difficult for the addict, he or she will do something to medicate the pain by taking an emotional aspirin (act out) to avoid dealing with the trauma from the past.

There are many pain agents (only four of which we will discuss here) that move the addict into the beginning of the addiction cycle. This cycle often starts with a shameful experience. In recovery, when the addict begins to understand this cycle, he or she will be able to short-circuit the necessity to act out.

A. Emotional Discomfort

Emotional discomfort is one of the primary pain agents that will move the addict to the first level of the addiction cycle and cause them to disconnect from their feelings. Emotional discomfort is basically a family of origin issue. The addict never learned how to identify feelings while growing up in his or her family. Consequently, many addicts have very primitive emotional skills. Therefore, when they have a painful feeling, they act out to feel better.

I remember knowing that when I felt any kind of emotional discomfort as an addict, whether hopelessness, anger, or confusion, I couldn't quite put my finger on it to identify it. Whatever uncomfortable emotional feelings I had, I knew that if I just acted out in some way, it would go away temporarily. The interesting thing about this is, it worked! My addiction did temporarily medicate and seem to relieve the emotional discomfort I was feeling. Emotional discomfort for many addicts is the pain agent that moves them forward into the next steps of the cycle of addiction.

B. Unresolved Conflict

Some addicts have been victims of physical, emotional, or sexual abuse and have unresolved issues about the abuse. Some have unresolved conflicts about their sexual identity or goals in life. Any kind of unresolved external or internal conflict can agitate the addict. It is this agitation that becomes part of this particular pain agent's unresolved conflict. The sense that *I don't have that skill mastered yet,* or *I don't feel good about myself because of that* can trigger the addict into the addiction cycle. These unresolved conflicts agitate the addict, which is the beginning process for the cycle of addiction.

An example of a trigger point for this unresolved conflict might be growing up in a physically abusive home and having unresolved issues around the abuse. When addicts have unresolved conflict, they act out as a way to avoid, minimize, or medicate this conflict. This can show up in their personal or professional life. For example, the addict may have an argument or misunderstanding with someone at the office and act out as a way to make themselves feel better due to their unresolved conflict.

C. Stress

Something we cannot avoid is stress. All of us have stress at some point in our lives. The way an addict medicates or avoids stress is by acting out. After the addict acts out, the stress seems to dissipate. However, the fact that the addict acted out creates more stress. This becomes a cycle for them as they keep adding stress to the pain agent, and then repeat the cycle again and again. Many addicts set up these dynamics in which they repeat this behavior by creating stress so that they can alleviate the stress again by acting out. Crazy? I know!

Addicts experience stress in several areas of their lives. It can come from the realm of their vocation. It can arise from financial pressure, as many addicts have difficulty budgeting money. Stress can be tied to close relationships, family of origin, or children. It can be about spiritual issues. Just the everyday grind of driving through traffic can be stressful for some. Stress—pressure from outside—can move the addict into a pain agent and back into the cycle of addiction.

D. A Need to Connect

Every human being has a need to connect. I believe that everyone is born with a need to touch and be touched, to be seen, and to behold others. Many addicts act out as a primary way of being satiated inside. It is through this altered state and false nurturing that the addict feels like he or she is connected. This can be very confusing for the addict in recovery since experiences of acting out in the past have all been a way to connect through his or her addiction. This need to connect can move the addict into the addiction cycle if he or she doesn't find other ways to enjoy the true way of meeting the need to connect. I have found that when addicts feel this need to connect, they also feel pain because they don't know how to get this relationship need met. The addict is faced with the pressure to act out in order to make the pain go away.

II. Disassociation

A common clinical term used in the treatment of addictions and traumas is disassociation. Disassociation simply means that the addict disconnects from himself, and often from God. Many addicts disconnect while driving. Disconnecting is a way that many sexual abuse victims survive from the pain of their past. These victims most likely disconnected during their trauma as well. Disconnecting while growing up in a dysfunctional home may have been a survival tool in that unsupportive environment.

Disassociating or disconnecting is the very beginning of the cycle, yet is still a separate stage of the cycle of addiction itself. Disassociation is necessary for putting the addiction cycle in motion. I compare this to an airplane traveling down a runway. There is a distinct time when the plane is on the ground and another distinct time when it has lifted off the runway and disassociated.

Disassociation is important to understand because at that very point we can use behavioral techniques to get grounded. Getting grounded can be as simple as making a phone call or going to a support group. It is while the addict is disassociated and not yet in the addiction cycle that he or she may still have enough sanity to keep the plane on the ground before it takes off to the next level, which would be the beginning of the cycle of addiction. This is crucial for addicts to understand so that they can be aware of when they are checking out and not totally available.

Many partners or spouses of addicts complain, "You aren't listening to me," or "You are not here with me; where did you go?" Friends and family of the addict are usually aware when the addict is disassociating or disconnecting and not really listening. This is a common experience for the family of an addict. The spouse of an addict may often feel kept at a distance.

Disassociation is the stage that follows after the addict feels past or present pain. The addict needs to do something with the pain, so he or she disassociates. Then he or she enters into the beginning of the cycle of addiction.

III. The Altered State (Fantasy World)

Another clinical term we use for trauma survivors and addicts is "altered state." Moving into the altered state is what the recovery community calls "the bubble." The bubble, or the altered state, is a place the addict may have created during childhood or adolescence that he or she identified as a safe place. Some people even have names for the place they go, though many addicts are not as sophisticated as this, and the altered state is simply a place to "check out" or fantasize. It is a place where the addict creates images or behaviors to begin to medicate.

The altered state can be very appealing and soothing. It is an emotional oasis that the addict may have created thousands of times. It can include pornography or fantasies about other people, even though they may not have actually had any affairs.

The altered state can be the emotional salvation for the soul's desert. For the workaholic, it's like getting a new job. For the sex addict, it's like getting a new relationship. For the spendaholic, it's like getting bigger and better toys. For the substance abuser, it's like getting a new beer or drug. The altered state temporarily eases their pain. It's the fantasy state that precedes the behavior and projects the behavior forward which will be helpful for them in some way to relax, escape, medicate, or just numb out any real emotions.

The altered state is where the addict goes to emotionally and cognitively check out of reality. It is similar to the analogy of the plane. The addict has his or her pain agent, the plane is on the ground, and then he or she decides it is too painful to handle alone. So the plane takes off and begins to climb to a cruising altitude. The addict enters the altered state when he or she reaches the cruising altitude and the plane levels off. The addict is now in a different reality. In this reality, the addict believes he or she is in total control. This is a very important part of the addiction cycle. Once the addict has entered the altered state, if he or she doesn't make phone calls to someone to whom they can become accountable or pierce "the bubble" somehow by getting back into reality, he or she will move into the next level of the cycle of addiction.

IV. Pursuing Behavior

Once the addict has achieved the level of the altered state he or she created in the bubble, he or she will then head toward a destination. There are sophisticated and unsophisticated ways of doing this. Nonetheless, a behavior will be pursued.

The pursuit of behavior can be very complicated. It may be pursued alone, with others or in fantasy. The addict practices specific repetitious behaviors and once he or she enters the altered state, he or she will be pursued and act out in some way. The addict is in pursuit, much like a plane going to its destination. He has gone from reality to fantasy, and now he is going to create whatever circumstances the altered state wants. The addict is trying to satiate something that is insatiable, even though he or she has experienced this many times. You and I both most likely remember this insanity.

During the pursuit, some addicts have specific places they go, people they see, or phone calls they make. Whatever their place, they are in pursuit of a repetitious behavior. For some, it may be a very clearly identified location. Some addicts have described it like this: "Yes, I was on my way to a particular place, and was totally out of control. I couldn't feel myself touching the ground at all." At this point, the addict has experienced all the physiological symptoms of being in the altered state and has pursued the behavior.

Pursuing the behavior is a very difficult stage to break unless you have the support of someone who can help you somehow pierce the bubble and get you back into reality.

V. Behavior

The behavior for addicts is repetitive and familiar. The behavior with each addict is different, but the experience is the same. Once the addict goes through the stage where he or she pursues a behavior, he or she continues by acting out. The addict repeats this behavior over and over again. Every time they go through this cycle and act out, neurologically and psychologically. They reinforce that the addiction is going to medicate their inner being. The reinforcement of this repetitive behavior is their way of dealing with pain and getting through stressors. This final behavior completes the cycle of addiction. This is where they "act out" as they say in Twelve Step groups. Those who are in support groups and continue to act out in one way or another won't get better. Their lives won't change if they continue to act out in any way within this cycle. They will basically continue to stay addicts. The best and only way you can stay free is if you don't reinforce the addiction cycle. This "acting out" behavior completes the cycle of addiction, except for one other item: Time.

VI. Time

I have counseled many addicts from various cultural and socioeconomic backgrounds, and there appears to be an individual pattern for each person. Knowing your pattern is key to your recovery.

Some addicts have acting out binge cycles. For others, acting out behaviors are further apart. For most, there seems to be a set time for the recurrence of pain and the actual acting out behavior. The time between one act and another may be hours, days, weeks, or months. There is time between one pain agent and another. Between these times, if the addict can incorporate their support groups, phone calls, and recovery, they can strengthen themselves. Then when the next pain agent comes, the addict can cope with it rather than giving himself or herself permission to act out because of the pain.

Time is a tricky issue. The time between acting out behaviors is your best opportunity to cope before the cycle starts. Pain will come into your life, and you can't control that. However, you can control what you do with your time so that when the emotional discomfort, unresolved conflict, or need to connect comes along, you can have the strength to say no and do something healthy with it instead.

As an addict, you need to feel the pain and stay in reality. Find positive behaviors to reinforce that you have value and are worth recovery. You and your family are worth recovery so that you can live a full life physically, emotionally, and spiritually.

Time can become your best friend. The longer the time between your acting out behavior, at any level, the better your life can become. Without support, time can be the only thing that keeps you from your next acting out experience. I would encourage you to memorize your own patterns of pain, disconnecting, altered state, and pursuing behavior.

I have observed this cycle of addiction in many addicts over and over again. This cycle is based upon new findings and research, since the first cycle was published several years ago. My encouragement is to identify where you are and to move on in the time you have today to recover.

If you fall down, get up and get honest. Christ does forgive you and has given you the power to overcome by connecting and being honest with others in your Recovery for Everyone group.

#6

Five Commandments
of Recovery

An Early Plan for Recovery

There are some basic principles that can help sustain your recovery from addiction. Early recovery is not simply understanding the facts, nor is it simply talking about addiction. Recovery goes much deeper than talking about what was done in the past.

Let's discuss what I call the Five Commandments of Recovery. These five commandments are simple and can be used much like a checklist that you would put on a wall or mirror at home (or use our app), where you can see it all the time. You may want to write the commandments down and check them off when you complete them. This is an ideal behavioral checklist for the recovering addict. It assures you that you are putting behavior toward recovery like the prodigal son; consistent daily behavior rather than just coming to an understanding about your addiction.

Coming to an understanding is not the only answer for the addict. They may have been in pain for years before and possibly repeated some behaviors hundreds or thousands of times. It is for this reason that the Five Commandments of Recovery, when put in place, give the addict an action plan they can use to begin to arrest the addiction they have been struggling with for so long.

Commandment #1-Morning Prayer

Prayer is something that many addicts early in recovery find difficult to do, especially if they have been avoiding God because of the shame and guilt of their behavior (or possibly because of what was done to them in the past). Consistent prayer at the start of the day is simply a behavior that can change the addict's disposition.

From all of the addictions medical science has studied, we know that an addiction is basically "self-will run riot." This expression of addiction simply means, "doing your own thing." First thing in the morning, put aside time to pray. Don't do your own thing. Do Commandment #1 instead.

You don't have to pray long. You can say, "God, I'm supposed to pray. I want to recover. Would you help me stay sober today?" From that point on, you can also discuss any issues you want to talk to him about. He is able to handle hurt, anger, fear, anxiety or any other feeling or thought you have kept from him. Prayer is a way for you to behaviorally change yourself. See it as a positive step in your recovery as well, as it makes you like Jesus, who is ever interceding for you in prayer.

For many addicts, addiction starts early in the day—not necessarily first thing in the morning, but perhaps during the drive to work. Prayer is preventative. It is a way of acknowledging that you have addiction issues and are in desperate need of sobriety. Without sobriety, you are on a path to self-destruction and you'll probably shatter other's lives as well. More than likely, those around you have already been devastated, either through your anger, depression, or acting out behavior. As an addict, you are in a fight every day, especially the first thirty to ninety days of recovery; typically the toughest period of recovery for the addict. Make sure you pray.

Prayer may or may not make you feel better instantly, but if you consistently apply it to your life, you will begin to reap the benefits. Prayer is one of the tools you will have as a believer who is a recovering person.

Commandment #2—Phone Calls

Making a phone call can be the very thing that saves you from an acting out experience today. The first step of the Twelve Steps talks about the word "we." "We" means that you need someone else in your program to help you. Do you remember what we covered earlier, about healing being in the body of Christ? In the past, "I" was the biggest focus in the addict's world. Before recovery, the addict was powerless. In being powerless, he or she couldn't fight addiction alone. The addict needs to involve others in the fight for sobriety. Having someone else involved dissipates the energy that comes against the addict. We cannot deal with addiction alone. I have not experienced addiction recovery alone and maintained not only abstinence, but a lifestyle of sobriety. Nor have I met anyone who has. When you are not alone, you are accountable. A lifestyle of sobriety is a much greater goal than just being abstinent.

There are several ways to address this commandment of making phone calls. One way is to wait until you get into crisis and then call someone to help you. This method does not work, because if you don't have a relationship already established with anyone, you have essentially set up a barrier that isolates you. To make a phone call and say you have addiction issues is a big enough task to accomplish. Calling someone you haven't established a relationship with and telling them of your plight is an even bigger task. It's likely you won't make the call at all.

The best way to utilize Commandment #2 is to make one phone call in the morning to another recovering addict, preferably someone in your Recovery for Everyone group. Tell them you are a recovering addict and that you are not in trouble, but that if you get in trouble during the day, you are going to call them. By doing this, you are checked in with someone. Eventually the phone calls will turn into conversations that develop recovery relationships. We need relationships, and part of our resocialization is making phone calls, feeling connected, and getting acceptance right at the beginning of the day. If you can make a phone call to someone else in the program early in the morning, you will find the strength you need to succeed during your day.

Like prayer, the phone is a tool you can use to help yourself grow stronger, especially within the first 30-90 days, when your need for other people to help is the greatest. The people you call will benefit just as much, if not more, when you call them.

Make a phone call to someone else in recovery every day. Again, this commandment as well as the others, is something you can put on your checklist each day. You don't need to philosophically agree with this concept or have a good feeling about it to decide if you are going to do it. This behavior is designed to help you get sober today and stay free.

Commandment #3-Reading

Reading recovery material specifically related to your addictive behavior is important. There are many books on the market you can read. It is very important to read some material every day. It is most beneficial to read in the morning. Addicts need to be reminded of what may be in store for them each day. Sometimes, what you read will come to mind in a difficult time. Recovery thoughts you glean from your reading can be the very tools you need to get out of your tough situation; giving you the strength to fight it. It is important to involve your mind in your recovery. Your mind alone will not save you, but it may help you to behave so that you can maintain your abstinent behaviors and not cross the line you have drawn. Go to www.Christianbooks.com or Amazon and search your addiction topic for material options.

By now, you probably have a feeling that your morning routine is going to change. These commandments take five to fifteen minutes. They can make a dramatic change in your day. Remember, no matter what you've believed in the past, you are worth getting the recovery you need so that you can restore yourself, your family, and your friends. You are going to learn a lot, not only about yourself, but about recovery in general. By doing so, you can successfully integrate into a lifestyle of hope and help others get free as well.

Commandment #4-Go to Meetings

"There are three times when you should go to a meeting: when you don't feel like going to a meeting, when you do feel like going to a meeting, and at 8 o'clock." This is a popular Alcoholics Anonymous expression. It is not a matter of how you feel about it. It is how you behave about it: you go to meetings. (Remember what we covered about kingdom verses democracy.)

In Twelve Step meetings there is a "ninety meetings in ninety days" rule. This rule is ideal. I counsel with addicts all over the country, and I know that in most major metropolitan areas, there are meetings almost every day of the week for some addictions, but not all. Weekly Recovery meetings should be your minimum goal.

Meetings are basically meant to support you, while at the same time, allow you the opportunity to give to others what you have learned through your own personal journey of recovery. Being around other recovering addicts who are getting free is going to help you. First, it is going to give you increased hope as you see others with various addictive issues move from bondage to recovery. Second, you may believe that if they can do it, you can too. You can learn many things from others in recovery that they have learned through their own negative or positive experiences. I want to encourage you to go to as many meetings as possible.

If you don't live in a metropolitan area, and can't get to meetings, it can be more difficult for you when you're in a tough situation. An alternative could be getting together frequently with someone of the same gender you've met at a meeting. This will give you support and a relationship with someone who can help you. The bottom line is, you need to be in as many meetings as possible.

I realize some of you reading this don't live in an area where there are groups. I also know some of you might perceive your social status to be at risk if you walk into a Recovery meeting of some kind. In my office, we have several independent counselors who have groups for addicts and even for intimacy anorexics.

These groups are work groups. You are expected to follow the Five Commandments of Recovery and do work in the *Recovery For Everyone: Steps* and *Recovery For Everyone: Workbooks.* You are expected to call the other members of your group just as you would if you drove across town to go to a meeting. I have found these groups to be tremendously helpful if you don't have a local group or you travel out of town quite a bit.

These principles were established with Dr. Bob and Bill W. in the founding of Alcoholics Anonymous. For information on their development, you can get the video; *My Name is Bill W.*, starring James Garner. You will be encouraged by how these principles have worked for more than sixty years with addicted people worldwide. We can help one another if we can get together. If you isolate yourself, you can't be helped—nor can you help others. Some days, you will be the one who needs help, while on other days, you'll be used to help other addicts (which is a great feeling). This is recovery. When you give this gift away, it reinforces your own recovery.

Commandment #5-Pray Again

This may sound like work because it is. You can read Commandment #1 again to remind you that this is not something you have to like or agree with; it is something you just have to do, behaviorally. At the end of the day, if you are free, pray a prayer of thanksgiving for a day of sobriety. Sobriety isn't something you do by yourself; it is something you do with the help of God and others. If there are any other issues from the day you want to talk to God about, you can bring them up in the same prayer. It is important to end your day in a spiritual place in addition to starting the day this way.

The recovery program that is going to work is spiritual in nature. Since you were born a spirit, with a soul, living in a body, it is important to reestablish your own walk with the Lord. Make this a time of being thankful that you had a day of recovery. Even the worst day in recovery is something to be thankful for, because even on the best day without recovery, you were covered with shame, guilt, and fear. So, if you have any relief from those feelings, I believe it is appropriate to pray and thank Jesus for all he has done for you so you could be free.

Unconditional love is something we rarely get in our lives. When we do get it, it changes us. Unconditional love is often a part of Recovery for Everyone groups. The other addicts in the group have been where you are, and are loved by others who have been there. Now that you are there, you can receive the love they have for you. When they stand up to give you a hug, it may feel uncomfortable at first, but let it happen and receive the love that they have for you. As one old-timer said, "It sounds like you are one of us." The acceptance and unconditional love you will receive from this group is something you may not have known you needed. It will feel like a weight has been lifted off you when unconditional love comes your way. Many addicts have not been loved for who they really are. The group is a place where you can be unconditionally loved because they know you and accept you just like you are.

Practicing these Five Commandments of Recovery and attending group meetings can allow you to see others who are reaching recovery. If you need to locate a group, go to our website, www.drdougweiss.com, and click the link for groups. My hope is that you can give this to yourself and inspire others who are on the journey to recovery.

#7

Soul Recovery

There are several goals to keep in mind in the soul recovery of an addict. In this chapter, we will explore some of the major aspects of the soul healing process. The first of the psychological processes deals with soul dependency in addiction. As covered earlier, the addict often becomes psychologically dependent on his or her addiction. I sometimes refer to this as "the first spouse." In his or her developmental life, this is the first place the addict discovered his or her needs could be met.

Psychological Dependency

This exercise from the *Recovery For Everyone: Workbook* crystallizes what an addict gets from his or her addiction from a soul aspect. Here's the exercise: Write a thank you letter and a goodbye letter to your addiction. First, the addict needs to look at what the addiction has done for him or her. It has often kept him or her from being responsible or intimate in relationships, justified him or her in leaving relationships, kept the him or her feeling powerful, loving, always in control, and successful in the addiction. In your letter, thank your addiction for what it has done for you from your adolescence, early adulthood, and all the way to the present. This will give you a good idea of the psychological dependence you have on your addiction in the past.

Second, you will write a good-bye letter to your addiction. This will give you a point and time when you confronted the psychological dependence, which has actually been a relationship you established. It has been a real person you have clung to in your fantasy world of addiction. Some have even crystallized this person specifically. It is now important to face the psychological dependence of the addiction so that you can also confront the issues. From this letter you may be able to deduce some of the other issues you need to deal with as far as the psychological dependence. If the dependence was for escape or entertainment, you are going to need to look at those issues and make a plan for legitimately meeting those needs in another way. We do need to have fun, entertainment, and be loved in a healthy way. Your addiction was there oftentimes to compensate for those needs not being met. In recovery, it will be your responsibility to identify these needs and find a healthy process for meeting them. The first aspect is to deal with the psychological dependency. This letter will be a beginning for this and again, you can refer to your *Recovery for Everyone Workbook* for further details.

Family of Origin

For many addicts, the family of origin is a complicated issue. A majority of addicts grew up in homes that were dysfunctional, and they may have been dysfunctional in many different ways. Their family could have been neglectful to where the addicts weren't invested in, praised, or celebrated. Another way their families might have been dysfunctional is that other addictions were active in their homes, such as food, nicotine, work, or sex, which made the environment the addicts grew up in very distant and emotionally absent.

Children from this kind of environment grow up without skills to deal with life's stresses and issues. Such children are then left to decide which addiction they will choose to medicate the absence of those skills and/or the pain of the distance within the family.

There is also the more abusive, angry, or volatile family system that can produce an addictive person. Abandonments could be in the addict's family of origin, including divorces where one of the parents leaves. The child is then susceptible to psychological pain, which is one of the pain agents for addiction.

As you look at your family of origin, you may find causes for issues you are dealing with. How did your parents deal with anger? Did they show love?

In this chapter we are just highlighting the psychological aspects that need to be addressed during treatment. Individual therapy may be needed while looking at these issues. If there is a lot of pent-up anger which can show up in either the form of either depression or hostility toward mom or dad, this will need to be addressed in your recovery process. Anger is held within your body and keeps you in pain. From the psychological aspect, to recover from addiction, you will have to heal your mind, will, and emotions that are hurting because of neglect, abuse, or dysfunction in your family of origin. If this is a large issue for you, seek qualified professional help.

On the other hand, some addicts grew up in an ideal situation. They are biological addicts who don't have family of origin issues to deal with. But they will still need to do quite a bit of work, though not in this particular area.

Feelings

This is a major part of addiction recovery. During our development years, many of us did not learn to identify or communicate feelings, and yet feelings can be one of the most treacherous and dangerous areas in our early recovery. Many addicts have at some point felt unloved, rejected, or unappreciated, which puts them into a difficult place if they don't know how to express their feelings. As a way of dealing with feelings, many addicts end up medicating through an unhealthy sexual activity. In any addiction, I find that feelings are something that addicts don't have much skill in fully expressing. This is just an issue of the lack of a particular skill. It is not a matter of a level of intelligence.

In the midst of the addiction, when an addict had a feeling and didn't know what it was, when they acted out, it went away. It was a simple solution. However, in recovery, you don't have the solution of acting out. You have the problem of having a feeling and not knowing what it is.

The following is an exercise that can help facilitate this. It is called the Feeling Exercise. If you need more explanation to complete this exercise, you can find it in the *Recovery for Everyone Workbook*.

1. I feel _____ when _____.

2. I first remember feeling _____ when _____.

This exercise is difficult at first. It's like learning a new computer program. Although it may be frustrating, you will get familiar with it eventually and then wonder how you lived without it. First, we identify the feeling. Without doing this part of the exercise, you can't do the second part, which is communicate. In the appendix, you will find a feelings list. Pick a feeling word from the list and fill in the blanks.

For example:

1. I feel calm when I go to the lake with my friend.
2. I first remember feeling calm when I was playing with an electric train set my mother bought me.

In this example I am giving a picture. These are to be very specific experiences. What we are doing is creating files. Our emotions as addicts are similar to a messy desk. We are taking the papers off the desk in this exercise and putting them in a filing system that goes a, b, c, d, and so on. In computer language, it's like having a database without file names. If we look for a file by name, we can't find it. This makes the addict feel like he or she doesn't know what to do, think, or feel, and so he or she acts out. Being able to identify feelings is very important. Do this exercise daily for about three months so that your verbal language increases. Write them down and you will be able to experience some feelings. After your first thirty days of abstinence, you are going to find yourself having some feelings. It is important to realize what you are feeling so that you don't relapse.

The second part of this feeling exercise is communication. You can do this exercise with a therapist or with someone in your recovery group. You will need to communicate the feeling sentences you have completed. I encourage you not to do this over the phone. Some may want to do this exercise with their partner or spouse. If you do this with your partner or spouse, it is important that you do NOT use your relationship in any way, shape, or form as examples. An example of what NOT to do:

"I feel frustrated when you don't pick up your socks." You can feel frustrated when you drive down the highway or when the dog sleeps in your favorite chair, but don't aim it at your partner, and don't use the word "you." This is the only way this exercise should be done with your partner, otherwise it will lead to another way to battle each other. For more guidelines here, see your *Recovery for Everyone Workbook*.

If this exercise is done correctly, it can provide a safe place for you to communicate your feelings. While one person is sharing his or her feelings, the other can listen. The person listening shouldn't make comments on the feelings shared for seventy-two hours. This creates a sense of security for both to know they are safe to communicate their feelings. This exercise will accelerate moving you from feeling frozen to feeling thawed. This exercise will be like sitting in the microwave, emotionally. Without this exercise, I find that addicts seem to have more relapses, and it also takes a lot longer time to develop intimacy, which we will discuss next.

If you are really interested in moving your emotional development forward, I highly recommend my book *Emotional Fitness*. It can take anyone, addicted or not, from emotional weakness to emotional strength. The exercises in It provide a road map to better identify, communicate, feel and even intelligently switch feelings.

Intimacy

In early recovery, the addict is unable to become intimate because his or her feelings were still frozen. He or she did not have the skills necessary to be intimate. Intimacy is the result of having the skills and emotions. Because the addict has been medicating their emotions for so long, they are underdeveloped. The addict is really unable to develop the kind of intimacy a lot of people experience, and that their spouse may want from them. If you are in recovery, intimacy is an obtainable goal for your future.

Intimacy is basically the ability to be able to share your heart, feelings, or deeper part of yourself with another human being. You will sense feelings of acceptance and love, mutually. It has sort of a spiritual aspect to it. You will feel connected, close, and warm. In their development, addicts have learned not to share with people because of a lie they believe: "If you knew me, you wouldn't love me." Consequently, many addicts have not experienced intimacy, so they don't believe it exists. They need to grow past this. You can practice intimacy and get better at it. This takes months, but as you practice sharing and being honest, you will experience intimacy. You'll begin to add to your experiences. The more experiences you have, the more you will believe and accept the existence of intimacy. This is an integral part of your recovery.

Trauma

Trauma is common to most addicts. It may have been emotional, spiritual, physical, or sexual abuse and/or neglect. Trauma comes in many shapes, sizes, and forms. It is a very important piece in your psychological recovery. In this book we are unable to go into great detail about trauma, since it could be a whole book unto itself.

Being a victim of trauma, abandonment, and neglect, I have had to work through trauma personally and it has been healing to do so. After about forty-five days clean in recovery, I find my clients are ready to work on their trauma issues. You will need to have your feelings in place before you can deal with trauma.

There are techniques you can use to address trauma. First, identify what your trauma was. As you go through your feelings, you may go through some recall of what has been traumatizing to you. As a person whose feelings are frozen, you may not realize what your trauma actually was, but as you thaw out in your recovery, trauma may become more obvious to you. As you complete steps four and five, you will find more information that will lead you to believe there has been trauma in your life.

When you identify the trauma, make a list of the incidents so you know what you are going to be dealing with. You may need a competent professional to help you through your trauma issues. Be sure to read the section in this book on how to find a therapist for your trauma work. Also, you'll find cognitive exercises and writing exercises to help you work through the trauma in the *Recovery for Everyone Workbook*.

I believe that if you deal with trauma early in your recovery, you will be more successful in your recovery. Without it, you keep the psychological pain. With that pain, you keep the drive to medicate within you. This is not what you need to do to yourself.

You are worth recovery, and having the best life possible. However, you will need to open up the secrets you have kept inside. If you have secrets, it may be that they are trauma secrets. Secrets can keep you sick and in your addiction. If you are keeping a trauma secret, it is important that you get honest. For example, many addicts have been sexually abused by older women or men and don't call it sexual abuse. I have had clients who could not acknowledge this as abuse, and as a result, ended up expanding the length of their acting out considerably. Once you have identified these traumas, you should begin working on them.

You are worth recovery! It may be hard work at times to peel through some of the layers you might have but you are worth that recovery in your life.

#8
Good Grief

Grief is a natural process human beings work through to naturally move through pain. One painful reality could be the death of a loved one. The pain of that loss is often overwhelming, so the process of grief allows us to take pain in increments or stages. We will cover the stages, but first we will explore how addicts grieve. Addicts go through the grieving process at several levels, over several different issues.

As the addict recovers, he or she grieves over the addiction. I would like to express addiction as a multifaceted relationship. It is a biological relationship. Often our addiction has been there all our lives. It has been there to run to and nurture us, and it has been our primary route to false intimacy. It has been with some addicts ten to fifty years, and often was their first experience of meeting a need or medicating pain in their life.

Addiction is often a loss of a relationship you can no longer have. For many addicts, it is the loss of a best friend. Losing your best friend can be painful. In all honesty, all of our relationships outside of recovery are usually secondary relationships. The secret life was primary. When you count up the hours the addict typically spent in their addiction, you find that addiction has absorbed thousands of hours of time. So to say good-bye to a friend who has been there all the time, every time, is difficult. Nonaddicts will not understand this relationship, just like others don't understand what it is like to lose a parent unless they have gone through it themselves.

In going through this grief of losing a primary relationship, you may not meet people who understand, unless they are people in your Recovery for Everyone group who have also gone through the grief and loss of a significant relationship. Your new life without addiction can be very scary. Avoiding grief is a way to avoid this change and growth. Grief is a way to help us experience and move through the pain of our loss. By moving through it successfully, we can enjoy the rest of our lives with other primary relationships, such as our spouse, children, and friends.

The Loss of Our Image

Our image is what we present to the world. For addicts, that is about 90 percent of our lives. We project an image of sometimes being very competent, strong, intelligent, successful, and often almost perfect. An addict I had in treatment once said that when he came into recovery, his wife said to him, "How am I going to accept you as being imperfect? I'm used to relating to you as being perfect." Often there is overcompensation for being an addict. We feel we have to be more than human, so we project a nearly perfect image to our peers, coworkers, family, and friends. In this way, addicts try to cope with and hide their addiction.

Losing an image that we have crafted and perfected is quite a large loss. It is the loss of self as defined by our addiction. This loss of self can be just as large as the loss of addiction. It is the loss of who I am to the outside world and now I am redefining that through recovery.

It is similar to what children go through with their parents. When they are young they think their parents are wonderful, but when they get older, they think they are terrible. As adults, they realize their parents were just people. We ourselves are going to go through these kinds of phases. Just realizing that developmentally we are human beings makes us realize we have flaws and strengths. We don't have to pretend. We can relax and "be," instead of trying to perform an image for others and base our acceptance on this performance.

Our loss of image is significant. There may also be reciprocal grief as far as the loss of our image to others because they also depended on our image for their own purposes.

The Loss of People

As addicts, we may have related to other people in our addiction in unhealthy or even ungodly ways. The losses of some of these relationships can be very painful. Indeed, we have overidealized our relationships, and in our early recovery, it was very difficult to separate the fact that our relationship was based on addiction. The loss of places where we received social reinforcement in our previous acting out days is also a part of the loss. These are losses we are going to incur early in our addiction recovery only because we have depended upon these structures and our addiction to survive. I use the term "survive" and not live, because an addict has only just begun to live as he enters recovery. In a lot of ways the addict has only experienced a limited amount of what life has to offer, so now in recovery, he or she will have to go through the grief process.

Grief Stages

The stages of grief were outlined by Elisabeth Kübler-Ross as she worked with those who were dying of cancer. These stages have been applied to many aspects of life, such as losing loved ones to death, divorce, or injury. Loss of a primary relationship, such as an addiction, is important to discuss.

Stage One-Shock

Shock is a feeling you experience when you are initially confronted with a painful reality, such as acknowledging you are an addict—especially if you are already a "Christian." The first time it was mentioned to you, for a moment, you may have been struck by the realization: "What am I doing?" That was shock. Shock is a feeling that is beyond communication, but you know when you have experienced it. I have seen many addicts experience this stage in my office as they discover the truth about their addiction.

Stage Two-Denial

To deny something means you have a "knowing" on some level that it is true. You can't deny something unless you know that there is some validity to it. So denial is a defense mechanism which allows us not to see or feel or connect with the truth of what is real. For example, if someone died, we might say they are not dead. In that case, we would hope denial would not last a long time. Unfortunately, in the case of addiction, denials can last for years, and in some situations, can lead a person to death.

Denial can be so great in addiction that it can kill. This is a defense mechanism which allows them to maintain their addiction.

Many addicts have numerous ways of denying their addiction before they come into an acceptance of being an addict. Some denial statements are: "Everybody does it"; "I didn't lose my job," or; "I'm not hurting anybody." Denial is a great way of saying, "I'm not what I know I am." This can be contagious in a family system where everyone agrees that you are a wonderful person, so no one there confronts your denial.

Denial is usually broken by one of two methods. In one method, denial is broken when the pain inside becomes so great that you experience the reality that you are an addict. In the second method, it is broken when you experience getting arrested, being threatened by divorce, or getting caught in an act of your addiction.

Denial is a phase that everyone goes through. The Twelve Steps help a recovering addict stay out of denial. Having people who love us enough to see our denial is important for any addict. If denial has been an issue for you in your more rational moments, express the kind of denial statements you have to your support team, your sponsor, group members, or spouse, so they can reiterate it to you during your denial. Denial is tricky, and when you reenter it, it will lead you to a path of destruction back into your addiction.

I have seen some addicts decide that they are not really addicts, only to finally realize that they are. Some have incurred serious consequences from going back into their addiction. My encouragement is that if you are in denial about any part of your addiction, then share what you are thinking with others who are serious about recovery. Believe what other people are seeing more than what you are saying.

Then there is religious denial: "I can't be an addict. I'm saved and filled with the Spirit." This is really crippling to the addict, especially in the wake of all the bad choices and pain they have caused themselves and others. "It's under the blood" is a common religious denial, again focusing on forgiveness rather than healing, like we explored earlier.

"I can't be an addict. I am a new creature in Christ," some protest. This one is almost laughable, at first. Let me see. You got saved and your eye color, hair color, and height stayed the same, but Jesus radically changed all your neurology related to your addiction and eradicated your abuse or family of origin history? This can be religious denial keeping this person from the very path of recovery which would allow him or her to have the process miracle of recovery and actuality live a life in which Jesus really did completely heal them of their addiction and brokenness. In your recovery groups, you will occasionally have a religious person share these ideas. It has been my experience that they usually do this due to stubbornness, laziness, or just unwillingness to do the work. Be patient and remind them that their ideas got them there, and that they may want to experiment with other ideas that will help them be free their entire life.

Stage Three-Anger

Anger is a good stage of grief. Anger indicates we are finally interacting with the painful truth that we are actually and factually addicted to something—some process or person. We don't like pain. It is uncomfortable and we are mad. We are mad that sometimes life has chosen to give us limitations. We are mad that we can't act out the way we used to or be with the people we were within the past. We are mad that a disease such as addiction is being cut out of our life. We are mad that God has chosen to heal us (as crazy as that sounds, it's true). All of these things are a part of anger and grief.

As a recovering person myself, I wondered why others could have sugar and caffeine when I couldn't. Being angry about this is normal and shows that we are making progress. It is not a sign that we are going backward. Eventually the anger will go away (or at least not be as prevalent), as you go through the stages of grief.

If you feel like there is a need to grapple with the anger, you can write your addiction a letter of what it has done to you over the years. This will help you work through your feelings. You can write about how your addiction has kept you from intimacy, honesty, enjoying life, and productivity. Anger will also come up if you are a survivor of abuse, which may have been a factor in you becoming an addict.

Anger shows that you are connecting with feelings. If you find that you need further help with your anger, consult a therapist and discuss techniques you can use to deal with your anger so you can move to the next stage. Anger is important to manage for you to maintain recovery.

Stage Four-Bargaining

Bargaining is a stage of grief that involves an "if...then" logic. For example, "If _____ (something) had not been in my past, I wouldn't have become an addict," or "If I could stop doing this for thirty days, I wouldn't be an addict." The bargaining can go on and on. It is an attempt to try to shift the pain and manipulate it to fit into categories, while still not experiencing the full impact of it. There is no shame in going through bargaining as long as you know that you are bargaining with your addiction.

As long as you are going to your Recovery for Everyone meetings and keeping the Five Commandments, you are probably going to be okay. Allow some caring people to be aware of your statements and confront you when they hear them so that you can continue to move into acceptance. Being what you are is the most freeing experience you will ever have. Our limitations are there so that we cannot destroy our lives. Coming to that recognition is a part of grief. Again, this is a normal process.

Stage Five-Sadness

For the addict, sadness is going to hit when he or she has been sober over a period of time. When he or she starts experiencing feelings, one of them will be sadness. This sadness may be over the things lost because of addiction, the damages the addict may have caused, and the risks taken by him or her. Some will think perhaps that they are going into depression. It can and may affect you this way. Your eating, sleeping, and energy level may be disturbed. If this goes on for a long time, you will need to consult a therapist about it, but it is normal to go through this stage. You will experience some periods of crying unrelated to any significant event. You will feel vulnerable at times. You might find you are isolating yourself from others.

It is sad that we have developed and behaved the way we did. Experience the feeling of sadness and understand that it is okay to feel this way because you are close to the end of your grief process. There is no way of getting through the grief process without feeling this emotion of sadness. To recover, however, hope is just one more stage away.

Stage Six-Acceptance

Acceptance is more than an intellectual or philosophical agreement that something is true. Acceptance is an integration that something is true. I can know cognitively that someone is dead, but integrating that and behaving as if it were true is a clear indicator I have come to acceptance. In the case of an addict, it is someone who is behaving as if what he or she knows to be true is true. The addict is going to meetings and making phone calls. He or she has motivation toward recovery and finds creative solutions not to act out.

Acceptance is an awareness one is what God has allowed one to be created to be, though with a limitation in the area of addiction, and is willing to take responsibility for this. Our behavior is one part of how we show this. I will behave as if I am a recovering addict and will find the greatest recovery in behaving as who I am, as opposed to trying to create an image or system to cover up what I am. In acceptance, I will accept my addiction and other painful events that have happened in my life.

Embracing Grief

Grief is something you will go through in various levels at different times, so it is important to look at how we grieve. One way to grieve is resistant. Resistant grief is when we push against the process. We don't want to feel the pain. We aren't praying and asking for help with grieving or feeling the pain. However, the more we resist, the longer it is going to take.

Grief has no agenda of its own. It doesn't necessarily take one or two years. It is the disposition that we take with grief that determines how long it takes to go through the process. We can embrace grief and let it take us through the process of healing, or we can resist it and just let it stand by our side until we embrace it.

Embracing grief is coming to a place of knowing that recovery is a process of stages, that you are going through these stages and embracing them. If you are reading this book, you are probably already out of shock and probably working toward moving out of denial (and possibly further). Though there are more stages ahead of you, you should be congratulated. The new life of recovery is just ahead of you, so be encouraged. If you can embrace the process, you can expedite it to a certain degree.

Grief and Our Partner

Addicts are not the only ones who go through grief, of course. The addiction is not only a painful reality to the addict, but to his or her partner and family as well. In looking at the spouse of the addict, the grief process for them is different than the grief process for the addict. When the addict finds out he or she is an addict and breaks through denial, he or she usually has a sense of relief that this is what it is. This is known as the "pink cloud syndrome" and it can last anywhere from four to six weeks.

During this time, the addict feels so good that he or she has finally self-identified as an addict that it may be difficult to understand his or her spouse's grief. The spouse of the addict is experiencing some painful realities, such as limitations of being married to an addict and financial or social consequences of the addiction.

The spouse of the addict goes through a lot of pain. He or she is suffering the loss of who he or she thought the spouse was. The person the addict is and the person the spouse thought they were can be diametrically opposed. The nonaddicted spouse may have to go through grief to even begin to integrate all these realizations. When the spouse finds out about the addiction, he or she is not going to go through a long stage of denial (though some may). More often than not, the spouse already knew something was wrong and began to put together the pieces of times, events, and people.

The spouse will actually spend most of their time in the anger stage. This anger can last anywhere from six weeks to six months. They will be mad at what they have lost because of the pretty picture they thought they had, the security they had, or the feelings they've had of knowing who the addict was and trusting them. I would encourage you to encourage your spouse to get therapy if they need it. It is important for you to understand that their grief is real and this anger is not necessarily toward you as a person, but toward your addiction. Depersonalizing for you is going to be important so that that you don't attack back or do other things that are going to agitate their grief process.

A good tool for you as the addict to watch is a DVD called *Helping Her Heal*. Although this DVD is for men who have betrayed their spouses through their sex addiction, many of the principles are helpful for all addicts, so they realize what they have done to their spouses and how to help them heal.

Grief is a process for the addict, the spouse, and family members of the addict. This will be an up-and-down process, but if they are doing this journey of recovery with you, be thankful.

#9
Dangerous Deprivation

Deprivation is a state that an addict keeps himself in which deprives him from having legitimate needs met. An addict will often have several areas of deprivation in his or her life. This is an essential element to identify for a healthy recovery. For some, it is their pain agent. It is one of the ways they keep themselves in a state of need. Because their needs are not being met, they believe they deserve to act out. This is one of the ways the addict stays in pain so that he or she can rationalize his or her acting out behavior. This is a subtle area you want to address early in recovery; otherwise you will be in pain, which is the beginning of the addiction cycle. We will look at deprivation several different ways and learn how to prevent it so that recovery can be much more successful.

Social Deprivation

When an addict isolates himself or herself from others, it is social deprivation. An extreme case would be someone who has no friends and plods through life with his or her addiction. This usually happens in a later stage of the addiction. Most addicts who do this have low social skills because their social and emotional needs are being met only by their addiction. Social deprivation will keep you from having friends and getting your needs met by people. It robs you of good feelings about yourself and keeps you in a state of constant pain.

Social isolation can be a way of life for some. I have clients who never developed socially because of their addiction. It is necessary for them to work hard in this area of their recovery so that they will not be socially deprived and remain in the cycle of using addictive behaviors to compensate for this loss.

Spiritual Deprivation

Many addicts have difficulty spiritually because it is necessary to be intimate and to have a spiritual relationship with God. God is not afraid to interact with us. However, we may feel we should be afraid to interact with him. The guilt and shame of where they have been or what they have done makes it difficult for some addicts to relate to God in an intimate way.

Religion is easy for the addict to maintain because it serves as their front to keep others from questioning their lifestyle. Spiritual deprivation can leave the addict feeling alone and disconnected from others. This deprivation often makes the addict question what he or she is supposed to do, and even why he or she is here. This deprivation is important to work on in recovery because otherwise, the addict can say, "God doesn't want me," or "God can't use me." These are rationalizations. If you believe these rationalizations, you can disconnect because there are no consequences for your behavior. You won't have to face a loving God who grieves at your underdevelopment, pain, and abuses. You won't be able to sense his love and compassion because of your spiritual deprivation.

This is important to look at as you go through your recovery, especially as you go through your second and third steps. As one person said, "God hasn't moved; we did." Spiritual deprivation can be a way to rationalize addictive behavior.

Sexual Deprivation (Sexual/Intimacy Anorexia)

In understanding that sex is spirit, soul, and body in a marriage, many never get what I call the gold medal in sex. Some may get the bronze or silver medal. What is happening? When the addict isn't being intimate with his or her spouse, his or her sexual needs are not met. He or she still has the core belief, *If you knew me, you wouldn't love me.* This is especially true if the addict's addiction has really hurt his or her marriage (which is often the case).

Some addicts sexually deprive themselves with their spouses (sexual anorexia) and yet regularly act out sexually with themselves. They say they want sex frequently, but then only have it once every two to three months. They keep themselves in a state of deprivation of sex with their spouses. This leads them to rationalize that they are not getting sex with their spouses. However, they are not looking at themselves and their responsibility to be emotionally supportive, kind, and loving. They may not even look at the fact that at home, they don't pursue their spouse sexually. They make other rationalizations as well, thinking that since they are in pain they can rationalize, support, or justify acting out behavior, regardless of what it is.

If you are disconnected during sex, you are engaged in non-relational sex and your spouse won't want it. This also can set up sexual deprivation. As you mature in recovery, sex can also improve in your marriage.

Fun

Countless times I have asked addicts what they do for fun, only to see their amazed faces, as if to say, "What do you mean?" The concept of fun is foreign to many addicts. This is primarily due to the fact that most of their entertainment needs are met in their addiction. Their addiction is their "fun" outlet. You won't see other outlets for fun in addict's lives. The addiction has become the primary way they get their "fun" need met.

Fun is a legitimate need. Everyone needs to have fun on a regular basis. Without it, the joy of life, creativity, and spontaneity can grow dim, which can set one up for deprivation. The rationaliza-tion is *I'm not having any fun.* They may be working too much, blame the kids or their spouse, or blame anyone but themselves as to why they are not having fun. This deprivation is sometimes planned. As addicts maintain this for sometimes weeks at a time, it can move them into a binge of acting out behaviors.

Those who don't have much fun in their lives need to evaluate why they are keeping themselves in deprivation. We weren't made to be boring. As we look at our early recovery, we need to look at the aspect of fun as far as designing it and having it. Give yourself permission to experience it. If this is an area of weakness for you, I strongly recommend you read my book, *The Power of Pleasure.* This book will help you identify what brings you pleasure and how to get that pleasure in your life.

Love Deprivation

Being deprived of love is a painful experience. Because of their core belief, *If you knew me, you wouldn't love me,* most addicts don't believe they are lovable. Sometimes they loathe them-selves. When someone doesn't feel lovable and has convinced themselves they are not lovable, when real love comes around, they discount it.

Such deprivation can keep addicts in trouble. If we don't believe we are genuinely being loved by others (whether family or friends, boyfriends or girlfriends), we keep ourselves empty, even if others try to pour gallons and gallons of love into us: we've got the door closed. No matter how much love is around us, as long as our door is closed, we can't experience it. Without experiencing it, we don't believe it is true. Once we come to that conclusion, we are in a lot of pain because we are living without love.

Living without love is lonely, boring, and can be painful. These feelings and experiences lead us to a point of deprivation where we say, "Nobody cares, and I don't care." In response, addicts abandon themselves to their addiction. They do whatever the addiction pleases because in their addiction they can believe they are loved. In the altered state or fantasy world, they have conditioned themselves to believe they are loved unconditionally. This has nothing to do with reality.

Intimacy Deprivation

Intimacy is similar to love but has more to do with emotions and the ability to share one's heart. Our counseling center is named Heart to Heart because I believe we deal with heart-to-heart issues. Generally, addicts do not have the ability to identify and communicate feelings. They have what is called "frozen feelings." Only after addicts have been in recovery for thirty to sixty days do they begin to thaw out. It could take several months to master their feelings and embark on a journey of intimacy.

In the beginning, addicts do not feel connectedness, but instead have something I call "the glass wall" around them, which leaves them feeling as if they are inside while everyone else is outside. People can't get to them, so they are safe, but they can't get to themselves either, so they feel desperate. They don't know how to meet the needs of others and they feel inadequate. The lack of intimacy is deprivation because all human beings need to touch and be touched. It is important to get this need met through the recovery group and healing. You might want to read one of our marriage books: *Intimacy: A 100 Day Guide to Lasting Relationships, The Ten Minute Marriage Principle, The 7 Love Agreements,* and *The Miracle of Marriage* to help improve intimacy in your marriage.

Physical Deprivation

Addicts vary on physical deprivation, as it does not apply to all of them. Regular exercise is a way to reduce our stress, which is important because stress is a precursor to acting out for many addicts. This is where the acronym H.A.L.T. (Hungry, Angry, Lonely, Tired) comes into play. These H.A.L.T. feelings are some of the strongest, and they stress addicts out, which makes them more vulnerable to acting out. Physical exercise is one of the things addicts can do to keep themselves in good health and have a better attitude about recovery. Exercise will also help endorphins and enkephalins move in the brain so addicts have a steady influx of them rather than getting them from acting out behaviors. Exercise provides a healthy balancing opportunity. If addicts don't exercise, they can put themselves in a state of physical deprivation by continuing to work hard, staying up late, and making the body toxic.

As we explored earlier, pain needs medicine. Physical pain especially needs physical medicine. So, if you are not exercising, you are setting yourself up for physical pain. You will need to look at this aspect in your recovery and how you can meet this need and move along. We can see that many have unmet needs. It will take time to develop this in your recovery.

Financial Deprivation

Finance seems to be an issue for most addicts. They compulsively spend money despite being in debt and bearing the burden of that debt. The addict tries to pay off debt to compensate for this, but then end up needing to use credit cards to pay for groceries. This cycle is just one of many in which many addicts find themselves. They need to practice self-restraint by keeping a close eye on their budget and paying off debt.

Be sure to set aside entertainment funds so you and your partner can have fun on a regular basis. Set aside funds for Christmas gift buying and for going on vacations. Create a plan that is manageable and be accountable to someone for it.

The Importance of Deprivation

The reason deprivation is so important is because unawareness blinds many addicts. This blindness sets them up for a great amount of pain. When they are in that overwhelming sense of pain without knowing what they are feeling, they get confused. In that confusion, their addiction becomes the way out. The addict feels entitled to act out, and is tempted to do so. Then he or she is filled with guilt and shame from the consequences of the behavior, which sets them up again in the addiction cycle.

It is important to understand that deprivation is a prelude to pain, which begins the addiction cycle. If we can look at deprivation in our life and manage it, we will be less likely to be blindsided by pain. The addict needs to look further into the fact that he or she is the only one able to meet that need.

At one time, I remember specifically thinking that I didn't have many male friends in my life. I had acquaintances, but not deep friendships. I felt this was a legitimate need, so I made myself responsible for the need and came up with a plan. I thought of several men who had things in common with me and asked them to do something as a group, to see if we got along. Three very significant relationships developed. My need for friendship was met in those relationships. I had to look at my need and take responsible for it. "Always with Intimacy" When I made a plan and actively pursued it, the results followed.

The deception of deprivation is that if you stay in pain in major areas of your life, you will tend to believe the deception of negative rationalizations: *you deserve it, nobody cares, you're not loved anyway.* These are all lies, but you can't see this early in recovery because you have believed them for so many years. I can say now that I know I am loved and I don't have to hurt myself or my family, or be a victim. I now know I can have as much fun as I want, along with intimacy. You can too.

Look at this deprivation early in your recovery because the blindsiding effect of your deprivation can hurt you. Identify it and take responsibility for it and make a plan. Get accountable to the plan and you will find yourself in a better place.

Steps to Change Deprivation

1. Identify and check off the areas of deprivation that apply in your life.

- ☐ Social
- ☐ Spiritual
- ☐ Sexual
- ☐ Fun
- ☐ Love
- ☐ Intimacy
- ☐ Physical
- ☐ Financial

2. Identify the rationale to acting out. List as many of the rationalizations in these areas of deprivation as you currently believe you have so that you are aware of them when they come up in the future.

3. Identify patterns and the length of time or geography for acting out. Some addicts have 2-3 day, one week, or monthlong patterns. Some act out only when they go out of town, or their spouse or family go out of town. Make yourself accountable to your group, sponsor, or therapist.

4. Look at the areas of deprivation. Write down realistic goals and work to begin to meet those deprived needs. For example: fun. If you are a golfer, write down that you will play once or twice a month to start. Start off slowly and realistically. Let your sponsor, spouse, or therapist know your goals so they can help keep you accountable to them.

#10
The Twelve Steps

Now we enter into the recovery program known as the Twelve Steps. The original Twelve Steps were written many years ago for Alcoholics Anonymous. After some period of sobriety, these alcoholics decided to write down the principles and steps they took to maintain their sobriety and live healthier lives. These principles and steps have been used throughout the world to help millions of people with various addictions, such as narcotic abuse, overeating, emotional problems, codependency, and sexual addiction.

These steps are rooted in biblical principles. If you study the history of Alcoholics Anonymous, you'll find a lot of prayer was involved. In the 1930s, most Americans had a biblical worldview. The secularism and new age thoughts didn't exist in large measure back then. Your *Recovery for Everyone Step book* will guide you intelligently and specifically through each step in your recovery. The pages that follow will help you understand the basic concepts of these principles called the Twelve Steps.

The Twelve Steps of Alcoholics Anonymous
Adapted for Anyone

1. We admitted we were powerless over our addiction, and that our lives had become unmanageable.

2. Came to believe that a power greater than ourselves could restore us to sanity.

3. Made a decision to turn our will and our lives over to the care of God, as we understood God.

4. Made a searching and fearless moral inventory of ourselves.

5. Admitted to God, to ourselves, and to another human being the exact nature of our wrongs.

6. Were entirely ready to have God remove all these defects of character.

7. Humbly asked God to remove our shortcomings.

8. Made a list of all persons we had harmed and became willing to make amends to them all.

9. Made direct amends to such people wherever possible, except when to do so would injure them or others.

10. Continued to take personal inventory, and when we were wrong, promptly admitted it.

11. Sought through prayer and meditation to improve our conscious contact with God as we understood God, praying only for knowledge of God's will for us and the power to carry that out.

12. Having had a spiritual awakening as the result of these steps, we tried to carry this message to others, and to practice these principles in all our day to day living.

An Interpretation of the Twelve Steps for Everyone

Step 1

We admitted we were powerless over our addiction and that our lives had become unmanageable.

We. I am so glad that the first word in the first step is "we." I would hate to think I was the only person who ever went through this. Addiction is an international as well as national problem. "We" means that we have similar experiences and we are alike. We grew up in the same family, though thousands of miles apart. We had the same kinds of abuses and neglects. We is a comforting word in this step. You can see that you are not alone and don't have to be alone. You can get better if you decide to get together. We is an encouraging word and is also essential. Without each other, we often fail to recover.

Admitted. This is a difficult word. Many of us have had difficult situations in our childhood that we have had to admit. Maybe we stole something or something happened to us and we had to admit what we did. Do you remember those feelings of dread before you admitted some wrong you had done or another had done to you? In spite of that dread, we went ahead and admitted what we had done or what happened to us. After we admitted it, we felt less heavy or unburdened, and as if we could then move on. For the addict, admitting is one of the hardest things we will do in our recovery. Admitting is a very important aspect of recovery and only those who admit to addiction can move forward in recovery and life.

We Were Powerless. Again, I'm glad there is a "we" in there and that I'm not the only one who is powerless. When we talk about power, we talk about control. Authority, strength, or force can enable us to be over others. However, that is not what this word is. This word is "powerless." As we know, the suffix "less" means "without"—such as jobless. This is a tough reality for every addict. We are without any strength, power, control, or force to influence our addiction. This is why we need each other and a recovery program. Sometimes, that is why we need therapy: we are powerless. We have tried not to act out without success.

Our Addiction. This is our unique way or combination of ways we have chosen to medicate our lives and became addictive. Our addiction may be chemicals such as alcohol, drugs, sugar, or caffeine. Our addiction may be a process like gambling, working, or relationships. Regardless of our addictive behavioral choices, over time, we became addicted. These behaviors led us down a road of out of control behaviors from which we now desire recovery.

And that Our Lives. Our lives can be many things. They can be our physical, emotional, intellectual, or spiritual lives. If you look at all the parts of our lives, they wouldn't equal the totality of our lives. Our lives are the very core of us, the inner part of us that identifies us as being separate from others. This is what has been affected by our addiction. This is the part that feels disconnected, alone, confused, and isolated when our needs are not being met. It is about this part of us we are going to admit something very important.

Had Become. These two words indicate to me that this has taken a while. It means that it took time, energy, process, and choices. It didn't just happen. It took a while and then eventually, it was made. Your life didn't become overwhelming or devastated instantly, but over a period of time.

Unmanageable. When we think about manageable, we think about things being in order or serene. We can tell when we walk into a store, whether the store is manageable or unmanageable. This word means unorganized and chaotic. If someone came from the outside and saw it, they would say "What a mess!" Sometimes this is the way we feel, and our feelings can be valid. Many areas of our lives we have talked about have become unmanageable, unconnected, uncontrollable, and unpredictable. No matter how hard we have tried to make them look good or perfect, they don't and they are not. Our lives have become empty and hollow in many respects. Now, through step one, if we can admit this unmanageability, we have a strong hope of recovery.

I encourage everyone to take step one seriously because it is the foundation of the Twelve Step program. It will cause you to have a good house of recovery to live in for the future.

Step 2

Came to believe that a power greater than ourselves could restore us to sanity.

Came to Believe. Again, notice the step is written in the past tense. The original steps were written to share the process that the original members of AA went through in recovery. There was a process through which they came to believe.

It is really a simple process. You come to believe many things during your lifetime. For example, you came to believe that there was a Santa Claus. Later, you came to believe that there wasn't a

Santa Claus. As you grew older, you may have come to believe that a certain person liked you, and later realized they didn't like you. We come to believe certain religious and political positions. There is some consistency to this process throughout our lives. In this process, there is a definite point at which you understand or come to believe.

In Twelve Step groups, the process of coming to believe is something that often happens as a result of exposure to other recovering people. You may not necessarily know the date or hour when you did come to believe, but you know that you feel differently, and you begin to have hope. This is so important in recovery, because knowing that you have come to believe, or knowing you do believe can save your life. Addicts can get down, feel hopeless or worthless, experience severe shame and guilt from past traumas, or present circumstances and resort to sad behaviors of destruction, isolation, and acting out. If you have come to believe, you have hope that God cares for you, loves you, and accepts you.

A Power. "A" is a common word. You use it every day—a cat, a dog, a book—and in every context in which it is used, it denotes "one." If you were going to use a word to describe more than one, you would say "these," or another word that indicates plurality. This step is not written in the plural. It says "a power greater than ourselves." This is significant. Being an "a" here, you realize that there is one entity, one strength, one energy, one spirit—just one power. As believers, we know there is one power and his name is Jesus.

Greater than Ourselves. This is one of the first areas which require trust from the addict. We now know that there is one that is greater than ourselves. This is the best news we have in recovery: We don't have to figure this out alone. As you begin to trust Jesus, you begin to recover from the sick patterns, poor choices, and undesirable relationships that have been so much a part of your past.

Could. "Could" is one of the most helpful, loving expressions in the Twelve Steps. Could this power have the ability, the resources, the energy, and the intention of helping you along in the recovery process? It is possible now to begin to be restored. It is possible now to begin to be healthy, to have loving relationships with loving people, to be loved and nurtured in a healthy way. It can be done, and Jesus can do it. It is the experience of many in addiction recovery that if given the freedom and the opportunity—in other words, if they quit trying to do it all on their own—Jesus will do for them what they have been unable to do for themselves. All you have to do is ask and stay honest, and he will do for you what you have been unable to do.

Restore Us to Sanity. "Restore" means bringing something back. When one thinks of restoration, one typically thinks of restoring an automobile or an old house and making it look like new. The same is true of addiction recovery.

For so long, addicts have been robbed of spirituality, intimacy, trust, and even their own reality. In a world that should have been safe, we violated ourselves again and again.

Insanity is natural when you live with a disease as crazy as an addiction. You may have difficulty applying the idea of insanity to yourself, but most addicts share that having two lifestyles at the same time and living with the secret can make them feel insane. You try again and again to do something that should work, but doesn't. You try and try to fix the problems that an addiction creates in your life, without success.

The behaviors themselves are insane, but the fact that you use them again and again, never stopping to realize that they're not working, qualifies you to be restored to sanity. It is possible for addicts to be restored to sanity. Those already in recovery have experienced it. They are living proof that it is possible to make better choices, and as you read this, I hope you know this is possible for you. You may still feel crazy, but if you have gotten this far in your recovery, you have a good chance of finding sanity.

Step 3

Made a decision to turn our will and our lives over to the care of God as we understood God.

Made. "Made" is kind of like "became." It indicates a process which involves time and choices, but there is definitely a time when it is done. For example, when kids in school make an ashtray in art class, a meal or a dress in home economics, there is a time when it is in the process of being made, and then it is completed. It is made. "Made" is something that is finally resolved to the point that you can say it is done.

A. Here again, we come to that little word, "a." It is one. What is stated in step three is a onetime event. Many people want to spread this step out, but as you move along in this process of working the steps, you will see why we only make this decision one time.

Decision. When you make a decision you list the good and the bad, the pros and cons of a situation. In this step, you can make a list of what you have done with your life in the past, and how you could deal with your life differently in the future. Such a list makes it easier to make the decision you are asked to make in step three. It is a decision.

Compare it to a traditional courtship and marriage. Step two is like an engagement period, during which you make a commitment to share your life with God. You have a single ceremony, but it sets the stage for further development throughout the relationship. Step three asks you to be willing to share your life with God. This decision is a onetime event, but it provides a means for further growth. For some believers this is like moving Jesus from Savior to Lord of all your life.

To Turn. Turning can be expressed in many ways. Someone said once that turning means, "to flip over," kind of like a hotcake. The hotcake gets done on one side, and then you have to turn it over. This is a pretty simple definition of turn, but it is also pretty profound. If you flip over, you make a total turn or change from the way you have been up to that point.

"Turn" is used on highways all over the world to indicate direction. Signs may indicate a left or right turn, or a U-turn. When you make a U-turn, you turn around and go in the opposite direction. What you do in step three is definitely a U-turn! You turn away from your limited understanding of how life should be. You leave behind perceptions, experiences, and ideas about things you thought you understood. You turn from them and gain a whole new perspective. This is an essential part of recovery. You are turning into something, or turning somewhere else, and it is amazing how far that turn can take you as you continue in your recovery efforts.

The good news is you have Jesus with you in the turning process and you have others in recovery that have made this turn to encourage you as well.

Our Will. Again, this is plural, as the group stays and works together. In this group of safe people who have turned their wills and lives over to God, you will begin to see this decision as a possibility for yourself.

What is your will? The simplest definition of "will" is probably "the ability to make the choices you do for your life." In the group, you will begin to turn over to God the choices that you make. This can be an easy thing to do for some, but for others it can be a very hard thing. It means you must turn your choices over to God, try to understand God's perspective, and follow that perspective in your life. This is why step three is so powerful.

A common phrase used in many groups is "stinking thinking." Stinking thinking is the way an addict, alcoholic, or non-recovering person thinks. This thinking doesn't work. The choices non-recovering people make don't bring about positive results. There seems to be a certain self-destructiveness to their choices and behavior. Step three cuts to the core of stinking thinking. It is the beginning of a new lifestyle.

Giving up their will is a safety valve for addicts. In making decisions about relationships, they are now able to turn to God. As they do, God will demonstrate new directions they can take, and new choices they can make. They will begin getting answers and be able to make different choices about their addiction behavior. This is a recovery they gain only by letting go of their own will or choices and turning them over to Christ fully.

Our Lives. Our lives are the result of all our choices. For each individual, life is the totality of all parts. When you turn it all over—spiritually, emotionally, physically, socially, financially, and sexually—you give yourself to God. You begin to trust God. You begin to believe that God will take care of you.

You may consider this a frightening prospect and ask, "How can I trust God?" However, take a good look at what you have trusted in the past. You have trusted your own ability to think and your own ability to make choices. You have taken the advice of a few chosen people who have not necessarily acted in your best interests.

Turning your will and life over is necessary. It is through this trust experience with God that you begin to believe God loves you. You begin once again to trust yourself. Eventually, you can even regain your trust in people.

Step three is an essential part of working the steps. It is not a luxury. It is necessary for a healthy, happy life. Working the steps is not always easy, and often you do not understand why you must work them. Often the steps are understood only after they have been completed. Then you realize the beauty of this spiritual process and open yourself to further growth and joy as you walk this road with others who are making the same steps toward recovery.

The Care of God. What do you think of when you hear the word "care"? It is often expressed in terms of: someone who loves you; someone who demonstrates some kindness toward you; someone who is willing to get involved in your life, who gets in there to work with you and is patient and does not condemn you in the process; someone who can be nurturing. All these pictures of a loving parent or loving friend can represent care. We feel care in the release of energy from one person to another, usually through kind behaviors like providing a listening ear or some other expression of concern.

How does this relate to God? What is the care of God? It is simply God's willingness to be involved in a nurturing, supportive, accepting way in your life. God is concerned for addicts. God's concern for others in this world demonstrates that care. You can sometimes see it more clearly in the lives of others than you can in your own life. For some addicts, the group is a manifestation of the care of God in their lives. By looking at others in your Recovery for Everyone group, it is possible for you to connect with this issue in such a way that it radically changes your life. Something as simple as their support can be seen as the extension of God's care and concern.

Let's focus on God now. The original writers of the Twelve Steps changed only one word from the initial version. In step two they changed the word "God" to a "power greater than ourselves." That is the only change they made, and they made it for this reason: Those first alcoholics said that God was too scary for the recovering person in step two. Maybe the recovering person had too many hurts or too many problems with God. So they changed the word "God" to a "power greater than ourselves" to give the newcomer an engagement period that allowed them to experience God through the group's care, nurture, and love. In this way, the newcomer could come to believe in a caring God who could and would help them.

Who is God? Simply put, God is love. God is also in authority—in control—especially to those who turn their lives and will over to him and switch the authority from themselves to God.

According to what you have learned so far in the steps, God has the ability to restore you. God is more powerful than you are, either alone or in a group. God gets actively involved in your life, and he has more power and more success than you in dealing with addiction. This God can and will help you as you work the Twelve Steps.

As We Understood God. One way to interpret this is to compare your understanding of God with the way you function in relationships with people, because we are talking about a relationship. When you first meet someone, your knowledge of him or her is limited. Only over time and through communication and commitment do you really come to understand another person in a relationship. The same is true in your relationship with God: coming to understand him is a process. However, this relationship is available to any and all in recovery who are willing to turn their wills and lives over to him, allowing them to experience a new life, recovery, and find happiness. The beauty of finding Christ as Lord and Savior of all of you—even the addicted out of control parts of you—is awesome. Through the Holy Spirit, he will move into these areas as you actively make him Lord and huddle up with other believers trying to do the same as you: be free from addiction for the remainder of their lives.

Step 4

Made a searching and fearless moral inventory of ourselves.

Made A Searching. Searching holds the possibility of fun, but for addicts, searching can be extremely painful. When you search, you intend to find something. For example, when you lose your keys, you go searching with the intent of finding the keys. As you begin your search inventory, you are searching, you are scrutinizing—you are seeking with intent to find something that is quite significant.

In this context, "searching" indicates that you will have to expend some energy. This is the beginning of what is often referred to in the program as "action steps." You now begin to take action on your own behalf. Note that this step is also in the past tense. As you begin your inventory, you can know that others have passed this way before and have survived and gotten better. You are not alone.

Fearless. "Fearless" simply means without fear. This is the attitude with which you approach your moral inventory. Being fearless allows you to view your inventory objectively as you uncover the pain. You will be looking at what was done to you and what you have done to yourself and others.

Many of the experiences you will be looking at are extremely painful. For some, the painful experience was childhood sexual abuse, for others it was rape. For some, it will be something else that they would much rather not ever remember—something they might think they only imagined. Fearlessness will lead you to look at your own part in the sick relationships you have been in as an adult, and at the patterns that have repeated over and over in your life. You need to look at these things with an attitude of courage and bravery. You can do this because, in step three, you turned your will and life over to the care of a loving God.

Moral. "Moral" can be defined as right and wrong, categories of black and white, or good and bad. Something that is immoral could be defined as something that violates your conscience. As you look at your life in step four, you will look for things you've done that violated your conscience. For example, as children, many of us were told not to get a cookie. Though there might not be anything wrong with having a cookie, we were told not to, so it became wrong for us to have one. What did we do? We waited until our parents could not see, and took a cookie anyway. It probably tasted good, but we may have felt badly afterward because we knew we had done something wrong.

In step four, you will also be looking at how you were violated by others. Have you ever said to yourself, If they really knew me, they wouldn't like me, or If they knew I was sexually abused or raped, they wouldn't be my friend? The shame and guilt you carry from the actions of other people toward you can be overwhelming. Step four is designed to release you from that shame and guilt as you look at how your moral code has been violated by others.

It is wrong to believe that you are unworthy because of your past. In recovery, you come to know yourself and let others know you. Step four is about coming to know yourself, being honest with yourself about what happened, and then taking into account how it affected your life and where it leaves you today. In short, step four is an inventory. You will list everything that happened, even if it involved others and you were simply an innocent bystander, as in the case of your parents' divorce or the death of a grandparent or other significant family member. Such an event may not have had anything to do with your morals, but it did affect you emotionally.

Inventory. What are you to inventory in step four? You inventory your experiences because, as a human being, that is what you have on hand. You inventory your memory, for that is what God gave you to record your experiences. Many see this inventory as a life story. It is a process where you begin to see the truth of what you've done and what has been done to you. Some things will be negative, others will be positive. When a storekeeper takes inventory, he lists not only the things he wants to get rid of, but the things he wants to keep. He doesn't just make a mental note of it, he writes it down.

Step four is a written assignment. You will need to have a pen or pencil, paper, and a quiet place to go to do it without interruption. Some just begin writing. Some organize their inventory by ages, such as zero to six years, seven to twelve years, and so on. Still others have do it by first listing all the traumatic events they can remember—things that were done to them or by them that violated their value system—and then write how they felt at the time, and how they feel now about those events. There is no right or wrong way to write an inventory. The important thing is just to do it. Perhaps for the first time, you will be face to face with the total reality of your life.

It can be pretty overwhelming, so don't be afraid to let your sponsor or therapist know how you are feeling while writing your inventory. As you transfer your story to paper, you are also transferring the pain, guilt, and shame onto paper. Writing an inventory can be a very positive transforming experience, and it is vital to your recovery.

Of ourselves. Once again, you can see this is plural. You can know and find assurance in the fact that others have done this before. You can survive the pain of writing your inventory down. It is joyous to see others freed from their shame. As you see other members of your Recovery for Everyone groups complete their inventories, you will begin to believe that this release from shame can happen for you too. You are reminded that only you can do this for yourself. Only you know your pain, the strength of your fears, and your deepest secrets. Only you are qualified to write this inventory. Now is the time to decide for yourself who you are, and who you want to be. There is great freedom in taking your focus off what is wrong with others, and doing a searching and fearless moral inventory of yourself. You may not understand the value of this step until you have completed it, but it is well worth the pain and tears.

Step 5

Admitted to God, to ourselves, and to another human being the exact nature of our wrongs.

Admitted. Here you are again, looking at that word, "admitted." You already know that it means to "fess up" or acknowledge what is already true. You may have already experienced the pain and joy of doing this, probably as a child or adolescent. Perhaps you put yourself in a situation you knew your parents would not approve of or did something wrong. You knew you were going to have to tell them, because you knew they were going to find out anyway. Do you remember your feelings of guilt and shame—that you had let them down as well as yourself? Then you somehow got the courage to tell them what you had done. You admitted the truth, no matter the consequences. It felt better, finally, to let the secret out.

The same is true in step five. You admit all that you have written in your fourth step. You let out all those secrets and finally feel that clean joy which comes from truly being totally known.

To God. God might be the easiest person to tell or the hardest. It depends on your relationship with him. If you feel God has let you down before, admitting what you've done wrong in life can be particularly difficult. Fortunately, God is forgiving of all that you have done and is willing to restore any lost part of you. As one wise person in recovery has stated: "It's okay to tell God. God already knows it all anyway. He is just waiting for us to be honest about it, too."

To Ourselves. Admitting your past secrets to yourself often takes place as you write your fourth step—if you are truly fearless and thorough when writing it. Admitting your powerlessness, your need to be restored to sanity, your profound amazement at your poor choices, and your sincere sense of having failed yourself all make this probably the most humbling experience you will have with regard to your sense of who you are.

It is at this point, though, that the recovery of your true self is able to take an upward turn, without the overwhelming sense of shame or guilt that has been so closely bound to you in the past. You are now able to begin a more shame-free life, which empowers you to experience the next and most essential part of this step: being able to reveal yourself to another human being.

And to Another Human Being. "What? I have to tell all this stuff to somebody else, face to face?" Yes, telling your story to another human being is the most crucial part of your recovery. In writing your fourth step, you have taken your total history of shame, hurt, abandonment, abuse and poor choices, acting out, and poured it consciously into one place. Your fourth step may even have brought to your conscious awareness some things you have been suppressing for years, and now all of these memories are in one place. If all that pain is kept inside you and not shared with another human being, you may talk yourself into believing once again that you are unlovable or unacceptable because of your painful, messy past. You could use this negative information and history for condemnation instead of healing. That is why we must tell another person. We must realize that we are loved and accepted even though we have been places and experienced things of which we are not proud.

In this fifth step you experience a cleansing or a lightening of your load spiritually, emotionally, and often, physically. As you share with another trusted person who you have been and what you have experienced, you are reassured that nothing you have done makes you unlovable. Someone knows the whole truth and still loves you. It is remarkable!

A note of caution is appropriate here: When you choose someone to hear your fifth step, it is important to pick the least condemning, most loving and accepting person you know. You might choose a therapist, sponsor, or spiritual person you trust. Choose someone who understands that you are digging into your past in order to make your present and future better—someone who will not shame you for your past. This person can be a member of your support group as well. This choice is yours. Make it in your best interest.

The Exact Nature of Our Wrongs. The fact that this part of the step is so specific will help two kinds of people: those who say, "I can't be specific, so I'll never really feel loved," and; those who believe they can own everybody else's wrongs and avoid looking at their own choices. The first person needs to be specific in sharing his story, because the shame he experiences about the past is tied to specific episodes. We must talk about those specific episodes to relieve the shame associated with them. The second person needs to acknowledge his own shortcomings and "clean his own side of the street"—not anyone else's—so that he too can be freed from his own shame.

It's a recognized fact that you can't free anyone else from their shame. Each person has to work their own program of recovery in order to have the kind of happy and fulfilling life we are all capable of experiencing. As a note of caution, for those who have violated children, most states demand that professionals report if the specific name and place of the event is given to them. Be aware of this when sharing this information as you do the fifth step.

Step 6

Were entirely ready to have God remove all these defects of character.

Were Entirely Ready. As you move from step one through step five, you discover a process through which you recognize powerlessness, find a God of your understanding, go inside yourself by writing an inventory, and let someone else know who you really are. The very core of the program is in the first five steps. By working these steps you have learned to "trust God and clean house."

Now that you have cleaned house, you must learn how to maintain your new surroundings. It is one process to clean a dirty house (whether you got it dirty yourself or just inherited all the mess) and another thing entirely to make sure that it never gets dirty again. That is what step six and the following steps are all about—preventative maintenance.

You start by "being entirely ready." This simply means that you are 100 percent ready to look at the damage done by all that trash, and you evaluate what you can throw away. You might be quite attached to some of that stuff. Even though it doesn't work any longer, you hesitate to give it up. *Someday, some of those old behaviors might come in handy*, you keep thinking. You forget that each time you try old behaviors they cause great pain. "Were entirely ready" indicates that you are finally tired of the pain. You finally realize that changing is not quite as frightening as staying the same.

To Have God. Having God in our lives is so significant for an addict. Here in step six they are reminded that like everyone, they are blessed by having a relationship with God. They are beginning to believe that God does want the best for them, and that God wants their lives to express this new way of feeling and believing about themselves. God is willing to work with you as you continue your efforts at recovery.

Remove ALL. This sounds like an unrealistic, possibly even painful statement, at least from a human standpoint. "Remove" indicates loss. Addicts have certainly experienced loss in their lives, but lose or remove all their defects? How? Well, it isn't up to you to decide how, only to be ready.

Remember that earlier you recognized that you don't have a whole lot of power of your own. In step six you will rely on God to have the power to change you—the power you've been unable to access in your addiction.

Defects of Character. As you consider the term, "defects of character," you might be thinking of some of the ways you have behaved and felt that didn't work very well. Go ahead and get a pencil and paper and write down what comes to mind. Reviewing your inventory should give you a good idea of things about your character you might want changed.

For example, perhaps the way you express your anger indicates a defect of character. Maybe you want to change things: the way you control and try to manipulate your spouse or children, pout to get your own way, or isolate or run away from responsibility for yourself. Honesty is important in listing these defects, because the ones you hold on to will keep you stuck in old patterns, and you will continue to attract unhealthy people into your life, especially in intimate relationships.

It is the experience of recovering addicts that as they become healthier and honest themselves, they gravitate toward more healthy, honest people, and are better able to determine who is unhealthy. Understanding this can certainly motivate you to really look at your defects of character, and be 100 percent willing to have God remove them. This is the real release that prevents the dust and trash from resettling in your house.

Step 7

Humbly asked God to remove our shortcomings.

Humbly. Many struggle with the word, "humble," having been humiliated time and again by the addiction. Humility is not the same as humiliation, although you may feel something like humiliation as you see the devastation in your own life and the lives of those around you caused by your defects of character. Humility, in this case, means recognizing your true humanness. You see in step seven the manner with which you should approach God.

Humility means knowing that you don't have the power to change yourself, but that God does. You come into God's presence with a humble heart, but with hope as well. As you ask, you shall receive. As long as you don't have preconceived ideas of just how and when God will remove your defects of character, you will have them removed.

Asked God. Humility requires that we ask God, not tell him. Perhaps by now you have come to believe that God really does want the best for you. He wants you to be free of your defects of character; feel good about yourself, and be attracted to healthy people. You are asking, in a sense, to do God's will.

To Remove Our Shortcomings. In step six, you became ready. Now you push the "Go" button and ask God to take your defects of character, or shortcomings. It would be nice if it happened all at once, but again, you will experience it as a process. In this process, God will be with you throughout your life, removing your shortcomings as you continue to identify them when they surface, as long as you are willing to ask for help.

For some addicts, this step comes easily. For others, it is very hard, especially if they are holding on, still rationalizing, still defending, and still gripping their defense mechanisms. In that case, step seven can be a painful experience. As someone once said in a meeting, "There was never anything I let go of that didn't have claw marks all over it, including my defects of character."

You can trust that if you ask, God will remove your defects of character, no matter how much you resist. If you decide to hold on to them, you will fight a losing battle. It is at this point that you will really need your support group. They will give you valuable feedback about any shortcomings they see you holding on to. If you aren't sure, ask questions. They will also give you support as you try new behaviors in place of the old ones that kept you so unhappy. Allow them to support you in this growth process.

Step 8

Made a list of all persons we had harmed and became willing to make amends to them all.

Made a List. You probably don't have any problem shopping for groceries if you've made a list. You know that the most efficient way to shop is to have a written list instead of just mental notes. Otherwise, you are likely to get home and find you have forgotten some essential items. There is a saying in Alcoholics Anonymous that you should be fearless and thorough from the very start. This is true in step eight. Again, take a pencil and paper in hand, and looking at your inventory, make a list of all those you have harmed. This list should include yourself as well as others, and can also include the damage that was done, and to whom.

Of All Persons. Here again is that sometimes scary word, "all." "All" means every single one. Once again, you are being challenged to be honest. To the degree that you can be honest in making this list, you will have hope for new relationships with important people in your life.

We Had Harmed. It takes an honest person to look at his or her life and see the people he or she has harmed. It is often easier to see how you have been harmed by others. In steps four and five, you looked at how you have been hurt by trusted people in your life, been traumatized, been emotionally abandoned, and how you have suffered. However, if all you look at is how you have been harmed, you are only halfway healed.

Just as it can be painful for a recovering alcoholic to see how his drinking damaged those around him, so it can be painful for the recovering addict of any kind to realize what he or she has done to hurt others. For many addicts, it is much more comfortable to be the victim. As a matter of fact, they have often been the victim of their own behavior, their own past, and even of recent relationships. Past victimization by others just makes it that much more difficult for these people to realize they have actually harmed other people. The acting out behavior is just the start of this list. The harm can be very subtle. You need to really search your mind and heart in order to complete your healing.

And Became Willing. The past tense here reminds you, one more time, that the hard work demanded in the previous steps is survivable. Addicts have worked their way through these steps before and found peace and happiness on the other side. It also indicates a process. Recovery doesn't just happen overnight. Becoming willing takes time for everyone, especially if one Is holding on to a victim status.

To Make Amends. What does it mean to make amends? For addicts (or anyone in recovery for that matter), to make amends means to acknowledge the wrong they have done, and be willing to be different. You stop blaming the other person to justify your own behavior. You stop rationalizing and defending yourself. You stop avoiding responsibility. You are continuing to change in your relationships with yourself and others. You take full responsibility for what you have done and those to whom you have done it (at least on paper at this point).

To Them ALL. Here is that word "all" again. It seems to appear everywhere throughout the steps. By now, your list should include everyone who has been harmed by your actions or lack of actions In any way. You should have found the willingness to be different with each person on that list, including yourself. No stone should be left unturned at this point. If not, you will still carry old guilt that will keep you stuck in old sick patterns of thinking and relating. With names, phone numbers, and accounts of damage in hand, you are ready to move on.

Step 9

Made direct amends to such people wherever possible, except when to do so would injure them or others.

Made Direct Amends. In step eight, you made your list. Now you go to the grocery store. In step nine, you actually go to the people on your list and make direct amends to them for your past inappropriate attitudes or behaviors that affected them. Notice again that this step is written in the past tense. These steps were written in the late 1930s when the first members of Alcoholics Anonymous became sober. Working these steps—especially step nine—was something they had to do to maintain their sobriety so they would not have to carry the pain, shame, or guilt of the past or present into their new sober lives.

They had to be honest with themselves. So do you as you go to each person on your list and ask them for their forgiveness. When you acknowledge how your behavior affected your relationships with them, you will find the most incredible recovery. As the result of working step nine, tremendous emotional weights can be lifted and relationships can often be restored. This is not a 100 percent guarantee, since some relationships will remain fractured. However, at least your side of the street will be clean.

You will begin to feel wholeness and happiness in your life now that you have made the effort to vent completely, without expectations. This is a significant point: You do not make amends with the expectation that your friends or family will change their behavior. You do not make amends with the expectation that people will respond in any certain way. People may, in fact, respond when you make amends, but it is by no means the motivation for you to do what you must to get rid of what you have been carrying for so long. Inflated expectations can cause you much pain because others are not always in the same place with their recovery that you are with yours. Many people do not choose a path of recovery at all. Your personal efforts and behavior, however, can challenge them into this kind of recovery at some point in the future.

It is not a given that the other person will ask forgiveness in return, even though they may have injured you much more than you have injured them. Your goal is to clean your own slate. You are not responsible for what others leave undone, nor can their shortcomings keep you from recovering and feeling good about yourself.

Except When to Do So Would Injure Them or Others. When you get to this point, you may become confused when you attempt to decide if making amends will injure the person involved or be detrimental to other (possibly innocent) people. Such confusion is best resolved with the assistance of a group, sponsor, or therapist. However, confusion is not to be used as an excuse to not make any amends because you don't want to experience the pain or shame of admitting your past behavior.

What you must consider when admitting past behavior is whether or not your confession would so significantly damage the other person involved that you should not raise the issue to them. You can ask yourself, "Would this be damaging?" If you have a question, do not assume you have the answer. You could very possibly avoid making an amend which could restore a relationship, or hold on to an amend that will set you up for old behavior. Go over your list with a sponsor, support group, or therapist, if at all possible.

Step 10

Continued to take personal inventory, and when we were wrong, promptly admitted it.

Continued. Here again you must deal with the maintenance of your newly clean house. You are not letting the dust fall. You are not letting the dirt collect or the garbage overflow the can. Here you are in a process, just as in steps four and five. Today, when you have been inappropriate or violated anyone's boundaries—including your own—you don't have to wait five or ten years to make amends. You can do it as you go along.

To Take Personal Inventory. Taking a daily personal inventory is a process through which addicts are able to look at each person in their lives and see how they interact with each one. They look at their attitudes toward others and honestly evaluate them. This is not done to the point where they are unable to enjoy interactions, but is an honest evaluation of how they respond to peers, family, and all other relationships. It is also a reminder that you inventory only your own behavior, not anyone else's.

And When We Were Wrong, Promptly Admitted It. You will be wrong. This part of step ten says "when," not "if" they were wrong. Many addicts have been wronged, but there will still be times when they are wrong. It is so important for the recovering person to stay free and not enter into a place of guilt and shame which can push him or her into some acting out behavior.

In the maintenance of step ten, when you are wrong, you prompt-ly admit it. "Promptly" is significant because it keeps you from holding on to the baggage, thinking for months about whether you were or weren't wrong. Promptly means admit it right now, right here. If you have been acting inappropriately, say: "I'm sorry. Forgive me. I'm acting inappropriately." It is as simple as that. Step ten gives you a way to stay free from the bondage of guilt and shame. It keeps you humble, which often helps you to remain healthy.

Step 11

Sought through prayer and meditation to improve our conscious contact with God as we understood God, praying only for knowledge of God's will for us and the power to carry that out.

Sought Through Prayer and Meditation. This step not only tells you what you are doing, but how to do it. You are seeking. You are looking to improve your relationship with God. This step tells you to do that through prayer and meditation. Prayer is that verbal (sometimes internal) communication with God. It is an incredibly positive experience for the addict to become more aware of God in his or her life. Jesus died so we could enjoy a relationship with him. This step lets you know that it is your responsibility. Seeking requires action on your part. You may have felt abandoned by God since you put no real effort into trying to find out where he was. In meetings it has been said many times, "If you can't find God, guess who moved." You move away from God—God never moves away from you. Seeking him is all it takes to find him.

Meditation is sometimes a deeper sense of prayer. Prayer is requesting, asking, interacting. Meditation is listening and hearing God's voice. A lot of humans experience rest and peace through meditation, and are able to still the constant obsessive thinking that prevents them from hearing what God has to say: that they are significant, they are loved, and they deserve to be healthy. Meditate on God's character, your personal relationship with him, some scripture or recovery material you have, and allow them to really sink in to your spirit. Be still and God will speak to you.

To Improve Our Conscious Contact with God. Like many people, most addicts have an unconscious contact with God. Most of the time, they rely on their own thinking and resources, and connect with God only after they have thoroughly botched their lives. Step eleven reminds you to keep God in your conscious mind. You are then able to experience the power and love of God in a whole new way. As a result, you will experience life in a whole new way. You will have a higher sense of purpose and joy.

The result of this new awareness of God on a moment to moment basis is a better relationship with God. As with any relationship, efforts at improving the relationship require time, energy, and some sort of communication. With time, you will find the method of communication that works best for you. There is no right or wrong way to do it. Just do it.

As We Understood God. It is impossible for any of us to totally understand God. The beauty of the program is that you can begin to see evidence of God in other people. Remember, this is not a job you undertake on your own. You come to a new understanding of God as you interact with the people in your support group or church. As you listen, you will grow in understanding through other people's experiences of God in their lives.

Praying Only For Knowledge of God's Will For Us. By now, you are beginning to see the benefits of letting go of self-will. In step eleven, you are gently reminded that when you pray for God's will in your life, you are asking for the absolute best solution to whatever you are facing. So often we push and push situations to turn out the way we want them to, only to find out that we got second, third, seventh, or tenth best. It is a very positive thing to realize that you can trust God to have your best interests at heart. The people, places, and things you have given your will over to in the past did not have your best interests at heart. You now trust God enough to say, "Not my will, but thy will be done."

And the Power to Carry That Out. You pray for knowledge of God's will, not just for the sake of having the information, but also for the power to carry it out. Having the information without the willingness or power to carry it out, will not change anything. After prayer for knowledge, you can listen in meditation for God to tell you the things you need to do. Sometimes a path will open. Sometimes God will bring to mind a defect of character that is getting in your way. Sometimes, through your intuitive thoughts or feelings, God will challenge you in the way you are behaving. Often the power to make the changes God seems to want you to make comes through the people in your support group. It can even come from seeing someone stuck in old behaviors. You can be motivated to change by seeing the consequences others are experiencing because of their unwillingness to act differently. Once having asked for direction and listened for guidance, you can act with assurance, knowing that if you are on the wrong track, you will come to know it. No matter what, you always know that you're not alone.

Step 12

Having had a spiritual awakening as the result of these steps, we tried to carry this message to others, and to practice these principles in all our day to day living.

Having Had a Spiritual Awakening as the Result of These Steps. It is no wonder that an individual who comes to the steps has a spiritual awakening. In the process of time, he or she admits to powerlessness, to humanness, and to the need for a relationship with God. He or she actively pursues that relationship, cleans house, makes amends, and maintains this behavior. This spiritual awakening is the purpose of working the steps. It is an awakening in which the addict discovers he has worth and value, and that he is loved by God and can be loved by others if only he will believe in his lovableness and open up his heart and let that love in.

This awakening to a spiritual connection with God can give the addict the power to change his way of relating to himself and the world. He can now see himself as a precious child of a loving God, and treat himself and others accordingly.

We Tried to Carry This Message to Others. In the beginning of Alcoholics Anonymous, it was not a matter of a drunken alcoholic seeking advice and support from someone who was sober. It was the recovering alcoholic who sought out the active drinker. Bill W., the cofounder of AA, knew that if he couldn't share what he had discovered about his relationship with God and its importance to his sobriety, he wouldn't be able to stay sober. This is true for any addiction. As you progress in your recovery and become less absorbed in your own pain, you begin to recognize when others around you are in pain. You will begin to see opportunities to share your experience, strength, and hope with other addicts who are suffering from the same low self-esteem, dependency and independency problems, and lack of boundaries you experienced. You will share, not to get them well, but to remain mindful of the miracle of recovery in your own life. Without constant reminders, you are likely to forget where your strength and health come from, and become complacent.

One of the truest sayings around recovery groups is, "You can't keep it if you don't give it away." The door to recovery is open to you because others passed this way before. It is your joy, as well as your responsibility, to keep the door open for those who follow you, and to lead them to the door if they can't find it. It is the only way to ensure freedom for all.

And to Practice These Principles in ALL Our Day to Day Living. Here is the most practical part of the Twelve Steps. Take what you have learned and keep doing it every day. Practice admitting your powerlessness over the problems in your life. Practice acknowledging God's ability to run your life and keep you from practicing old behaviors. Practice new thinking and behavior skills. Practice prayer and meditation. Like the athlete who must exercise daily to stay in shape, you need to practice daily the new skills you have learned, so you can stay in good emotional and spiritual shape. It took many years of practicing old behaviors for you to end up with such low self-esteem and such a lack of boundaries. It will take practice to become the new person you want to be, but it is possible!

Congratulations to all who embark on this journey of the Twelve Steps. When followed, these steps are a tried and true path to recovery from any addiction. Remember that you deserve the results of this work we call recovery.

#11
Professional Helpers

In addition to the vital attendance and involvement in Twelve Step recovery, many addicts benefit greatly from professional therapy.

What? Am I in need of therapy too? Does the idea of therapy frighten you? A general discussion of the types of therapy and treatment settings available might help you decide if therapy is for you.

A funny story from my own life illustrates this. When I first got saved, I was in a church that rejected all counseling and psychology, as they considered them to be "of the devil." This was the pastor's stance as well.

I was a brand new believer, just a month or so old in the Lord, I enrolled in Bible college. In the first semester, the school set our schedule. On my schedule, I saw I was registered for a psychology class. I was indignant about having to take this "secular" class.

I walked up to the dean's office of that small Bible college and "told" him that I wasn't taking a psychology class as it was of the devil. He was wise and told me not to worry about it, and that instead, I could take a sociology course later on.

God truly has a sense of humor. In seminary, he called me into counseling. I got a master's degree in marriage and family counseling and later, a Ph.D. in psychology. I never stop following Jesus, reading my Bible, praying or trying to be led by his Spirit in walking with clients.

God has called me into this helping field, so I want to explain It to you a little bit because it can be confusing to an outsider for sure. Here I'm going to walk you through a variety of types of counselors. This is so you can intelligently decide which type of help you might need.

Just as in the medical or financial fields, the mental health field has various levels of professionally trained people. These professionals have a wide variety of philosophies and training perspectives, and can meet different needs of addicts.

Counselors Certified to Treat Addiction

In most states, there are counselors who are licensed or certified as addiction counselors. Be very careful. Not all counselors who say that they treat addictions are actually licensed or certified to treat addictions. They should have letters after their name verifying they are a licensed addictions counselor of some kind. If it doesn't say "licensed" or "certified," before seeing them, ask them what qualifies them to treat addicts.

Not all counselors are Christians. This goes without saying. Not all people who advertise that they are Christians are actually practicing their Christianity. Ask the counselor for their pastor's name. Do they tithe? How often do they read their Bible? To whom are they accountable? If they are in recovery, from what are they recovering? (For how long?)

Psychiatrist

Psychiatrists are medical doctors. They attend several years of medical school and are trained to look at biological reasons for problems with human beings. They are trained in medications that influence the chemistry of the brain. This professional can be a valuable help or support to an addict who has been previously diagnosed with depression, manic-depression, or other problem that requires the supervision of a medical doctor. He or she can prescribe medication the addict might need to feel better, such as antidepressant medication.

If the psychiatrist has had addiction training, or has had exposure to workshops dealing with addiction, he or she may be of some help to you as you work on your issues.

Psychologist

A psychologist is quite different from a psychiatrist, although they are often confused, as they both have the designation of doctor. Psychologists are Ph.D., Ed.D., or Psy.D.'s, not medical doctors. They have not attended and graduated from medical school. They are not licensed physicians. Therefore, they cannot prescribe medication. They invest their educational training in looking at the cognitive (thinking) aspects of the human being, such as IQ (intelligence quotient), reading and math levels, psychological testing, and the like. He or she is often trained to do individual, group, and marital therapy.

A psychologist with a doctorate in psychology can be of great help to the addict, especially if he or she has had experience working with addicts. A psychologist can be of help to an addict in therapy, especially if the addict is experiencing any psychological disorder, such as depression, suicidal thoughts, or narcissism. Often these survival mechanisms respond well to treatment under the care of a trained and licensed psychologist.

Licensed Professional Counselor

The licensed professional counselor (L.P.C.) usually has either master's level training, or Ph.D. level training with expertise in counseling or another field (i.e. sociology or anthropology). They can acquire a counselor's license by taking certain counseling classes. A master's level degree is the minimum required for the L.P.C. in most states. The master's level professional may also have a degree in an area other than counseling, like an M.Ed. (master's in education), and take ten or fifteen classes in counseling during or after his or her graduate degree program, to acquire a professional license from the state he or she practices in. This is something to note in your initial interview with a licensed professional counselor. You can ask exactly what their background is, because in some states some licenses may not require a degree in counseling. This can be important for addicts to know when they are seeking help for their own issues or for the issues regarding their family, marriage, or children.

The master's level L.P.C., much like a psychologist, can be a great resource for a sex addict, as he or she deals with family and individual problems. An L.P.C. is usually able to identify and deal with depression, obsessive/compulsive disorders, addictive disorders, codependency, and other issues. L.P.C.'s like psychiatrists and psychologists have ongoing training and, in most states, will have a more reasonable fee structure for those seeking counseling. Ask the licensed professional counselor how many years they have been practicing and review the "Questions to Ask" section at the end of this chapter to determine their level of experience with addiction treatment.

Social Workers

Social workers will have either a bachelor's or master's level education. They may have several levels of certification, which can differ from state to state. They may be a certified social worker

(CSW) or a master's level social worker (MSSW), depending on their experience. Their training is mostly from a social perspective. Seeing issues from a social perspective is beneficial, and can be helpful, but if they have not been given specific training in the field of addictions, they may be limited in how helpful they can be. However, if there is a need for social services for the family or for the sex addict—for example, in finding places for residential treatment—a social worker can usually be quite resourceful. In some states, the social worker is much like a licensed professional counselor, as they provide individual, group, or family therapy. In other states and situations they may do social histories and things of that nature.

In finding a social worker, you will need to find out what educational training and experience they have had. You may find that this will be a very beneficial relationship to you, as you seek help for either your own issues or those of your family. Again, refer to the "Questions to Ask" section at the end of this chapter for further information.

Pastoral Counselors

Pastoral counseling is also available in many areas. Pastoral counselors include people who have professional degrees in counseling from an accredited seminary or institution. They may have a doctoral level education (Ph.D.), or they may have a master's level education. Pastors of local congregations would be included in this category. Although most pastors minimally have a bachelor's level education, some may have no formal education at all. Pastoral counselors can be very helpful in your recovery, because development of spirituality is a significant part of recovery for the whole person.

The strengths of a pastoral counselor would include his or her spiritual training, coupled with professional experience and professional training in the field of addictions, or counseling and psychological training. With such training, a pastoral counselor could be of the utmost benefit.

Some possible weaknesses of the pastoral counselor might be a lack of training or skill in some areas. The pastor who has had no training in counseling may be of brief support to the addict, but might not be as beneficial in resolving personal issues or identifying other psychological problems that an addict might have. Pastors are usually not trained counselors, but can be a great support to the addict in the recovery process of addiction as far as accountability.

The pastoral counselor, like all other professionals discussed, should be asked the appropriate questions from the "Questions to Ask" section. This is very important. Often, their understanding of addictions can influence how therapeutic they can be to you.

Christian Counseling

Christian counseling is another form of counseling which is now readily available in most large cities, as well as in some smaller communities. Christian counseling is not exactly the same as pastoral counseling. Many Christian counselors do not hold a position as a pastor, nor will they have professional pastoral counselor education training.

A Christian counselor is often professionally trained in the theory of counseling, psychology, and human development. These counselors can be master's or doctoral level trained professionals, but the training that the counselor receives can vary widely. It is wise to check the Christian counselor's training prior to having any therapeutic relationship.

There is a specific benefit in having a Christian counselor. They can be a great source of help, especially if they are able to integrate biblical truths and biblical understanding into the healing process. They can be very supportive and encouraging to the personal development of the addict, and can also facilitate growth for the whole family. Again, ask the questions relating to training and expertise in the area of addiction. Just because they are Christian does not guarantee they understand or successfully treat addiction.

Marriage and Family Counselors

Marriage and family counselors can have a variety of degrees in education also. They may have a Ph.D. or master's degree in marriage and family counseling. For addicts, this may or may not be helpful, depending on the situation. If you are in a marriage or a committed relationship, such a counselor can be very beneficial.

Marriage and family counselors come from a family systems approach, taking into consideration the needs of the entire family, and not just the needs of one person. Also, they will be highly attuned to how each family member processes problems, and how the family members interact with each other.

For example, in some addictive systems, the addict is the one who is perceived as needing help, the wife is the one who is strong and "helps" the addict, while the children are her supporters and cheerleaders in helping dad. From a systems approach, a counselor might look at this situation and say, "Dad needs to be sick so that mom can be a helper." Mom needs to give up the helper role and establish her own identify and boundaries, so if dad recovers, the family doesn't need somebody else to be sick (i.e., the children or mother herself).

The marriage and family counselor will be highly astute in these matters and can be beneficial to the addict, as well as to the family as a whole. Refer to the "Questions to Ask" section to determine what training and experience this counselor has in addictions in general.

It is very appropriate to interview the professional you are considering as a therapist. Each addict has a different history, and could have possible conflicts with certain professionals due to their past experiences. Also, the many professionals discussed here represent a sort of continuum of care. At one point in recovery you might find one type of professional more helpful than another. Many practices include several types of therapists and are able to treat sex addicts from what is known as a multidisciplinary view. In interviewing a potential therapist, consider the following list of questions.

Questions to Ask

- Do you have experience working with my type of addiction?

- How many addicts with my type of addiction have you seen in the last two months?

- Do you have training to do therapy with people with my type of addiction?

(Which state or board certification?)

- Are you a recovering person working a Twelve Step program?

- What books have you read on my type of addiction?

- Do you have specific training to deal with (if applicable to you) rape victims, survivors of child sexual abuse, incest, or other trauma?

#12
Recovery For
Everyone Groups

I want to take you on a journey I went through in working with addicts and their experiences in support groups. When I started treating addicts twenty-five years ago, the church almost universally had nothing for them. The only groups available were the traditional Twelve Step groups.

Twenty-five years later, the church is much more open to recovery, but what I have to share can be very helpful as to why the Recovery for Everyone groups are quite unique in the family of Christian recovery groups.

Many years ago, I sent my clients to the only groups in town. In many of these meetings, they didn't really check with each other as to how members in the group were actually doing. They didn't report on the step work they worked on. It seemed that what the group members did outside of attending groups and sponsor relationships was vague unless someone attended a group regularly for a while.

A person could stay on step one for years and relapses were common. The other concern in the group was a "no cross talk" rule, so you couldn't say anything to anyone in the group. One person at a time would talk. They might recite The Lord's Prayer together, but then the group was over.

Some of my brothers in recovery Christianized and adopted the entire secular model without question, and took those same weaknesses into the Christian recovery movement. Now remember, I have been in this movement for more than twenty-five years, so I have a longitudinal perspective.

Back then, my clients were not flourishing in these types of groups. I honestly evaluated the current recovery groups and went to work to create what I call a work group instead of the typical support group mode.

The following are done in the work group I developed:

1. Check-in includes what actual recovery work was completed that week. (Example: "I'm on step two and did Exercises 34-38 this week. I made seven for seven phone calls.")

2. After everyone checks in, there is a time for feedback, with permission. Joe says to John, "Can I give you feedback?" If Joe says "Yes," then John can give feedback to Joe. If Joe says "No," John says nothing.

3. The group has a topic which members discuss together.

4. Step work (Twelve Steps) is presented to the group and the group votes on whether they feel you have completed the step, or if it needs more work.

5. Sponsors are encouraged, but it's the responsibility of the person who wants a sponsor to initiate this.

6. For the first ninety days, group members are expected to follow the five commandments as much as possible.

These groups have worked for one of the toughest addictions out there: sexual addiction. These groups work all over the world, and I have seen thousands of men get free and stay free their entire lives, as well as partners and intimacy anorexic groups utilizing this same working group model. This model of recovery is not a Christianizing of a secular structure, but its own creation that is distinct, has proved itself over decades, and is being used cross denominationally with success.

What is a Recovery For Everyone Group?

A Recovery for Everyone group is a Christ-based working group for anyone with any addiction. This group has a format that fosters true accountability and provides materials that facilitate anyone getting free from their addictive behaviors or relationships, if they do the work.

Most importantly a Recovery for Everyone group is autonomous to the local church. There are no ongoing fees, national regulations, or authority structure. The pastor and elder of the local church are the authorities over the Recovery for Everyone groups.

This autonomy allows groups to choose their format for meeting that makes sense to their church community. These formats may include:

1. A large group meeting. After a short teaching, it breaks up into smaller groups.

2. A certain night for all the various types of Recovery for Everyone groups to meet in different rooms (i.e. alcoholic's room, a food addiction room, a codependent's room, a sex addict's room, and so on). They just all go into the small group format and do what they do well—get free together.

3. This is a cell group menu format where they meet all over the city. Topics and locations vary.

4. Any other idea that works.

I have only one fatherly piece of advice: Please keep your groups separated by gender. Recovery is an intimate process and early addicts are immature and may misunderstand this and act immaturely, hurting themselves and others.

Materials:
The basic texts for Recovery for Everyone groups are:

1. *Recovery for Everyone Book*
2. *Recovery for Everyone Workbook*
3. *Recovery for Everyone Steps*

Other books that are specific to each group's recovery focus are also used. There are so many books out there on recovery from almost anything that I wouldn't even want to start a bibliography. Besides, it would be outdated the moment it was printed.

Here again, consult with the spiritual leader over the church or recovery ministry; then go for it. The Recovery for Everyone materials are the foundational recovery material. Collateral reading is strongly encouraged.

Leadership

Recovery ministry is messy. This is where some of the most ugly and beautiful things occur, sometimes in the same meeting. Addicts do tend to create crisis, so this will be a normal event for the leadership to handle.

The reality is we are in a war with multiple addictions affecting believers in every church. To lead, you must really love people who at times don't love themselves. Have no need to be liked. Sometimes you'll need to speak a hard truth to truly show love. It will hurt them before it heals them. The leader must not be immoral or struggle with pornography (as this usually ends poorly), have his or her own recovery program, work well with crisis, be honest and have accountability, be in a consistent walk with Jesus, and have leadership affirmed by their church leadership.

I would also recommend that the leader do an assignment that given to me by my professors when I was preparing for ministry. I was to schedule a face-to-face meeting with a psychiatrist, psychologist, or other addiction counselor, and a polygrapher, just in case.

As a leader, you will meet people with real psychological or psychiatric problems. You need to know when you are over your head and know where to send them. For some people, recovery has more pieces to it because they are more broken than others.

Meeting Structure (Ideally)

1. The chairperson starts the meeting with a prayer.

2. Chairperson asks any first-timers to introduce themselves and state why they are present and if they are willing to abide by the Recovery Covenants of Confidentiality, the five commandments, and committing to meetings for a year.

3. Chairperson asks group members to do a quick check-in. This needs to stay short and structured, otherwise group members will waste a lot of time on unfounded conversation. The check- in should include:
    a. How long have you been free/sober?
    b. What exercises did you do this week?
    c. What step are you on?
    d. How many calls did you make this week.
    e. If you relapsed, did you do a consequence?

This really should take 1-2 minutes per person.

4. Chairperson asks if anyone has feedback. Remember that feedback is given with permission only. (Rob asks Frank, "Can I give feedback?" If Frank allows it, Rob proceeds. If Frank says no, Rob says nothing. The chairperson needs to be sensitive about what is being said and the spirit in which it it is said.)

5. Chairperson (or group member the chairperson has appointed), shares a brief topic for discussion. This should be 5-8 minutes so it doesn't become a monologue or teaching, but an invitation for other members to share their experiences or insights.

6. Group members discuss the topic. Try to let everyone share and be careful of anyone dominating in the group (including the chairperson).

7. Close in prayer.

This is the basic ideal structure. This allows quick accountability in the beginning, feedback, mutual sharing, and learning from each other.

Recovery for Everyone groups are a free market indigenous recovery ministry that any church can adopt. For those of you considering this very valuable ministry, I first want to thank you.

Second, I want to encourage you that as we heal believers of their addictions, they become powerful believers. I believe revival comes when the church is clean, honest, and healthy. These groups produce a DNA of healthy believers. I believe that Jesus looks forward to saying to you leaders and every person who takes this journey, "Well done good and faithful servant."

How do they work?

One man impressed by the Holy Spirit who wants to assist in helping others get recovery from being sexually driven asks his pastor to sponsor this ministry. This point man will be the contact person for the church. The church will refer to the point man anyone who feels sexually driven. This point man will meet with those desiring help and will cover the Recovery Principles and Recovery Covenant (see next page) with them. Once the person agrees to the Recovery Principles and Recovery Covenant, they are given the group location and time.

Recovery Group Roles

1. The point man serves as contact person for anyone to be brought into the group. This is to protect the group from someone just dropping in on the group. The point man can serve for an indefinite amount of time, but should be reconsidered after one year of service.

2. The chairperson of the meeting is responsible to start the meeting by asking the point man if any new people need to make a Recovery Covenant. If there are no new Recovery Covenants to be addressed, the chairperson starts the introductions (see Recovery Meetings) and chooses the topic for the group discussion. The chairperson serves the group for a maximum of 8 weeks. At that time someone else volunteers to chair the meeting.

Recovery Principles: First 100 Days of Recovery

1. Pray: Pray in the morning, asking God to keep you free today.

2. Read: Read the Bible and read recovery related material.

3. Call: Call someone in your group and check in with that person at the beginning of each day.

4. Meetings: Attend every meeting possible.

5. Pray: Pray in the evening, thanking God for keeping you free today.

One-Year Recovery Covenant

1. The members of the Recovery Group covenant to total confidentiality of all group members and discussions held during group meetings.

2. Members covenant to attend the Recovery Group for one year and to work through the Recovery for Everyone materials and report progress to the group.

3. Members covenant to keep the Recovery Principles for the first one hundred days of their journey toward recovery.

Recovery Meetings

1. Any new members are introduced by the point man and are asked to verbalize the Recovery Covenant to the group in the first person. (Example: I covenant to...)

2. Introductions: Beginning with the chairperson of the meeting, introductions are done as follows: The chairperson introduces himself, shares his feelings, shares his boundaries and length of time he has been free from those behaviors. (Example: "My name is John. I feel frustrated and alone. My boundaries to stay free are no pornography, bookstores, and no sex outside of marriage. I worked on Exercises 5-7 in my *101 Freedom Exercises* workbook and made four pages of progress on my *Steps to Freedom* workbook since our last meeting. I have been free for three weeks.")

3. The chairperson chooses a topic related to staying free from being sexually driven that the group discusses. Each member can share without feedback from the group, unless feedback is specifically asked for by the sharing member.

4. Honest Time: Group members pair off into 2-3 members and discuss thoughts, behaviors, struggles, and successes since the last meeting (James 5:16).

5. Closing Prayer: Group members get back together and repeat The Lord's Prayer together.

Recovery Group Materials

1. *Recovery for Everyone*—Within these pages you will find a tried and true path for recovery from any addiction. Here you will get a biblical understanding to break the strongholds in your life forever.

You will also find an explanation as to how an addiction may have become a part of your life and details as to how you can walk this path to recovery. You will find a roadmap to help you begin and navigate an incredible journey toward freedom. Then you can become part of the solution so that others can get free as well.

2. *Recovery for Everyone Workbook*—This workbook contains 101 proven techniques that Dr. Weiss has used to successfully help thousands obtain and maintain their addiction recovery. This is a great follow-up tool to Recovery for Everyone .

3. *Recovery for Everyone Steps*—This is a thorough interaction with the Twelve Steps of recovery. This workbook was designed to be used in a group setting, but can be used individually also.

These materials and others can be ordered from Heart to Heart Counseling Center, using the options listed in the Resource Section in Appendix D. Groups ordering ten or more of one item can call for a group discount.

Recovery Group Topics for Discussion

Triggers	Honesty	Fear
Hope	Bottom Lines	Relapse
Control	H.A.L.T.	Steps 1-12
Boundaries	Prayer	Maximized Thinking
Recovery Rituals	Feelings	Anger
Dangerous Dabbling	Fun	Father Issues
Sexual Abuse	Objectifying	Grooming Victims
Accountability	Discipline	Acts of Love
My Calling	My Future	Daily Struggles
Dangerous Places	What Works	Dating My Wife
Control	Male Friends	Humility
Turning It Over	God's Grace	One Day at a Time
My Daily God Time	Discipline	My Worst Moment
The Gift of Recovery	Intimacy	Breaking the Curse For My Children
What God is Doing	Exercise	Addictions in My Family

...And any other topic the chairperson feels is appropriate.

Remember, don't be graphic, be honest!

Appendix

Feelings Exercise

1. I feel (put feeling word here) when (put a present situation when you feel this).
2. I first remember feeling put the same feeling word here when earliest occurrence of this feeling.

Abandoned	Argumentative	Burned	Crabby
Abused	Aroused	Callous	Cranky
Aching	Astonished	Calm	Crazy
Accepted	Assertive	Capable	Creative
Accused	Attached	Captivated	Critical
Accepting	Attacked	Carefree	Criticized
Admired	Attentive	Careful	Cross
Adored	Attractive	Careless	Crushed
Adventurous	Aware	Caring	Cuddly
Affectionate	Awestruck	Cautious	Curious
Agony	Badgered	Certain	Cut
Alienated	Baited	Chased	Damned
Aloof	Bashful	Cheated	Dangerous
Aggravated	Battered	Cheerful	Daring
Agreeable	Beaten	Childlike	Dead
Aggressive	Beautiful	Choked-up	Deceived
Alive	Belligerent	Close	Deceptive
Alone	Belittled	Cold	Defensive
Alluring	Bereaved	Comfortable	Delicate
Amazed	Betrayed	Comforted	Delighted
Amused	Bewildered	Competent	Demeaned
Angry	Blamed	Competitive	Demoralized
Anguished	Blaming	Complacent	Dependent
Annoyed	Bonded	Complete	Depressed
Anxious	Bored	Confident	Deprived
Apart	Bothered	Confused	Deserted
Apathetic	Brave	Considerate	Desirable
Apologetic	Breathless	Consumed	Desired
Appreciated	Bristling	Content	Despair
Appreciative	Broken-up	Cool	Despondent
Apprehensive	Bruised	Courageous	Destroyed
Appropriate	Bubbly	Courteous	Different
Approved	Burdened	Coy	Dirty

Disenchanted	Friendly	Immature	Mean
Disgusted	Frightened	Impatient	Miserable
Disinterested	Frustrated	Important	Misunderstood
Dispirited	Full	Impotent	Moody
Distressed	Funny	Impressed	Morose
Distrustful	Furious	Incompetent	Mournful
Distrusted	Gay	Incomplete	Mystified
Disturbed	Generous	Independent	Nasty
Dominated	Gentle	Insecure	Nervous
Domineering	Genuine	Innocent	Nice
Doomed	Giddy	Insignificant	Numb
Doubtful	Giving	Insincere	Nurtured
Dreadful	Goofy	Isolated	Nuts
Eager	Grateful	Inspired	Obsessed
Ecstatic	Greedy	Insulted	Offended
Edgy	Grief	Interested	Open
Edified	Grim	Intimate	Ornery
Elated	Grimy	Intolerant	Out of control
Embarrassed	Grouchy	Involved	Overcome
Empowered	Grumpy	Irate	Overjoyed
Empty	Hard	Irrational	Overpowered
Enraged	Harried	Irked	Overwhelmed
Enraptured	Hassled	Irresponsible	Pampered
Enthusiastic	Healthy	Irritable	Panicked
Enticed	Helpful	Irritated	Paralyzed
Esteemed	Helpless	Isolated	Paranoid
Exasperated	Hesitant	Jealous	Patient
Excited	High	Jittery	Peaceful
Exhilarated	Hollow	Joyous	Pensive
Exposed	Honest	Lively	Perceptive
Fake	Hopeful	Lonely	Perturbed
Fascinated	Hopeless	Loose	Phony
Feisty	Horrified	Lost	Pleasant
Ferocious	Hostile	Loving	Pleased
Foolish	Humiliated	Low	Positive
Forced	Hurried	Lucky	Powerless
Forceful	Hurt	Lustful	Present
Forgiven	Hyper	Mad	Precious
Forgotten	Ignorant	Maudlin	Pressured
Free	Ignored	Malicious	Pretty

Proud	Scorned	Stuck	Understanding
Pulled apart	Scrutinized	Stunned	Understood
Put down	Secure	Stupid	Undesirable
Puzzled	Seduced	Subdued	Unfriendly
Quarrelsome	Seductive	Submissive	Ungrateful
Queer	Self-centered	Successful	Unified
Quiet	Self-conscious	Suffocated	Unhappy
Raped	Selfish	Sure	Unimpressed
Ravished	Separated	Sweet	Unsafe
Ravishing	Sensuous	Sympathy	Unstable
Real	Sexy	Tainted	Upset
Refreshed	Shattered	Tearful	Uptight
Regretful	Shocked	Tender	Used
Rejected	Shot down	Tense	Useful
Rejuvenated	Shy	Terrific	Useless
Rejecting	Sickened	Terrified	Unworthy
Relaxed	Silly	Thrilled	Validated
Relieved	Sincere	Ticked	Valuable
Remarkable	Sinking	Tickled	Valued
Remembered	Smart	Tight	Victorious
Removed	Smothered	Timid	Violated
Repulsed	Smug	Tired	Violent
Repulsive	Sneaky	Tolerant	Voluptuous
Resentful	Snowed	Tormented	Vulnerable
Resistant	Soft	Torn	Warm
Responsible	Solid	Tortured	Wary
Responsive	Solitary	Touched	Weak
Repressed	Sorry	Trapped	Whipped
Respected	Spacey	Tremendous	Whole
Restless	Special	Tricked	Wicked
Revolved	Spiteful	Trusted	Wild
Riled	Spontaneous	Trustful	Willing
Rotten	Squelched	Trusting	Wiped out
Ruined	Starved	Ugly	Wishful
Sad	Stiff	Unacceptable	Withdrawn
Safe	Stimulated	Unapproachable	Wonderful
Satiated	Stifled	Unaware	Worried
Satisfied	Strangled	Uncertain	Worthy
Scared	Strong	Uncomfortable	
Scolded	Stubborn	Under control	

The Twelve-Steps of Alcoholics Anonymous

1. We admitted we were powerless over alcohol–that our lives had become unmanageable.

2. Came to believe that a Power greater than ourselves could restore us to sanity.

3. Made a decision to turn our will and our lives over to the care of God as we understood Him.

4. Made a searching and fearless moral inventory of ourselves.

5. Admitted to God, to ourselves, and to another human being the exact nature of our wrongs.

6. Were entirely ready to have God remove all these defects of character.

7. Humbly asked Him to remove our shortcomings.

8. Made a list of all people we had harmed, and became willing to make amends to them all.

9. Made direct amends to such people where ever possible, except when to do so would injure them or others.

10. Continued to take personal inventory, and when we were wrong, promptly admitted it.

11. Sought though prayer and meditation to improve our conscious contact with God as we understood Him, praying only for knowledge of His will for us and the power to carry that out.

12. Having had a spiritual awakening as the result of these steps, we tried to carry this message to others and to practice these principles in all our affairs.

The Twelve-Steps of Alcoholics Anonymous Adapted for Anyone

1. We admitted we were powerless over our addiction—that our lives had become unmanageable.

2. Came to believe that a Power greater than ourselves could restore us to sanity.

3. Made a decision to turn our will and our lives over to the care of God as we understood Him.

4. Made a searching and fearless moral inventory of ourselves.

5. Admitted to God, to ourselves, and to another human being the exact nature of our wrongs.

6. Were entirely ready to have God remove all these defects of character.

7. Humbly asked God to remove our shortcomings.

8. Made a list of all people we had harmed, and became willing to make amends to them all.

9. Made direct amends to such people wherever possible, except when to do so would injure them or others.

10. Continued to take personal inventory, and when we were wrong, promptly admitted it.

11. Sought through prayer and meditation to improve our conscious contact with God as we understood Him, praying only for knowledge of His will for us and the power to carry that out.

12. Having had a spiritual awakening as the result of these steps, we tried to carry this message to others and to practice these principles in all our day to day living.

Counseling Services

"Without the intensive, my marriage would have ended and I would not have known why. Now I am happier than ever and my marriage is bonded permanently."

Counseling Sessions

Couples are helped through critical phases of disclosure moving into the process of recovery, and rebuilding trust in relationships. We have helped many couples rebuild their relationship and grasp and implement the necessary skills for an intimate relationship.

Individual counseling offers a personal treatment plan for successful healing in your life. In just one session a counselor can help you understand how you became stuck and how to move toward freedom.

Partners of sex addicts need an advocate. Feelings of fear, hurt, anger, betrayal, and grief require a compassionate, effective response. We provide that expert guidance and direction. We have helped many partners heal through sessions that get them answers to their many questions including: "How can I trust him again?"

A counseling session today can begin your personal journey toward healing.

3 and 5 Day Intensives

in Colorado Springs, Colorado are available for the following issues:

- Sexual Addiction Couple or Individual
- Intimacy Anorexia
- Partners of Sexual Addicts
- Partner Betrayal Trauma

Attendees of Intensives will receive:

- Personal attention from counselors who specialize in your area of need
- An understanding of how the addiction /anorexia and its consequences came into being
- Three appointments daily
- Daily assignments to increase the productiveness of these daily sessions
- Individuals get effective counseling to recover from the effects of sexual addiction, abuse and anorexia
- Addiction, abuse, anorexia issues are thoroughly addressed for couples and individuals. This includes the effects on the partner or family members of the addict, and how to rebuild intimacy toward a stronger relationship.

PRODUCTS FOR MEN'S RECOVERY

The Final Freedom
BOOK: $22.95/$35.00

The Final Freedom gives more current information than many professional counselors have today. In addition to informing sex addicts and their partners about sex addiction, it gives hope for recovery. The information provided in this book would cost hundreds of dollars in counseling hours to receive. Many have attested to successful recovery from this information alone.

101 Freedom Exercises
$39.95

This workbook provides tips, principles, survival techniques and therapeutic homework that has been tested and proven on many recovering sex addicts from all walks of life who have practiced these principles and have maintained their sobriety for many years. Jesus promised us a life of freedom, this book makes this promise a practical journey.

Steps to Freedom
$14.95

The Twelve Steps of recovery have become a major influence in the restoration of this country from the age old problem of alcohol and substance abuse. This book follows in the tradition of the Twelve Steps from a Christian perspective breaking down the various principles for each reader so that they can experience the freedom from sexual addiction.

Partner Betrayal Trauma
DVD:$69.95/COMPANION GUIDE:$11.95

The *Helping Her Heal* DVD paired with this companion guide are both vital tools for the man who has struggled with sexual addiction, exposed his marriage to the fallout of betrayal by acting on his urges, and is now seeking how to help his wife heal from the trauma of this devastating discovery.

Disclosure: Preparing and Completing
$39.95

This information can help the addict and the spouse navigate these often uncharted and misguided waters, saving the addict and the spouse from unnecessary pain or trauma. This DVD can expedite the understanding of each of the significant processes of disclosure for the addict, the spouse, and the marriage.

Healing Her Heart After Relapse
$29.95

This DVD is way more than, "He relapses, he does a consequence and moves on." The addict is given real tools to address the emotional damage and repair of her heart as a result of a relapse. Every couple in recovery would do well to have these tools before a potential relapse.

Boundaries: His. Hers.Ours
$49.95

Boundaries are a healthy, normal, and necessary part of the recovery process for sex addicts, intimacy anorexics, and their spouses. Implementing boundaries in a relationship may seem difficult, but with the proper tools and guidance you can successfully introduce and implement boundaries in your relationship. In this DVD set, Dr. Doug Weiss provides an answer to the clarion call on boundaries by educating and guiding you through this process.

Marriage After Addiction
$29.95

Addiction can have devastating effects on even good marriages. In this DVD you are intelligently guided through the journey you will experience if addiction is part of your marriage story. You will learn important information about the early and later stages of recovery for your marriage.

Series For Men

Clean: A Proven Plan For Men Committed to Sexual Integrity
BOOK: $16.95/DVD:$29.95/JOURNAL:$14.95

Clean is a priceless, no-nonsense resource for every husband, father, brother, son, friend, pastor, and Christian leader on the front lines of this war. It is a soldier's handbook for those ready to reclaim their homes, churches, and nations for the God who has built them to succeed.

Lust Free Living
BOOK:$13.95/DVD:$23.95

Every man can fight for and obtain a lust free lifestyle. Once you know how to stop lust, you will realize how weak lust really can be. God gace you the power to protect those you love from the ravages of lust for the rest of your life! It's time to take it back!

Men Make Men
DVD:$29.95/GUIDEBOOK:$11.95

Dr. Weiss takes the listeners by the hand and step-by-step walks through the creative process God used to make every man into a man of God. This practical teaching on DVD combined with the Men Make Guidebook can revitalize the men in any home or local church.

Addiction Recovery

Recovery for Everyone
BOOK: $22.95/DVD:$99.00/WORKBOOK:$39.95/STEPBOOK: $14.95

Recovery for Everyone helps addicts fight and recover from any addiction they are facing. Learn truths and gain a biblical understanding to break the strongholds in your life.

You will also find an explanation as to how an addiction may have become a part of your life and details as to how you can walk the path to recovery. You will find a roadmap to help you begin and navigate an incredible journey toward freedom. Then you can become part of the solution and even help others get free as well.

Secret Solutions: More Than 100 Ways to End the Secret
$39.95

Female sexual addiction is real and impacting many women's lives today. This Workbook is a practical step-by-step guide for recovery from this growing issue in our culture. The *Secret Solutions*, can be used in conjunction with therapy or as part of Twelve Step relationships or groups you may be a part of. My hope is that you receive the precious gift of recovery as many others have, and that you maintain it the rest of your life, for your benefit and for the benefit of those you love.

PRODUCTS FOR PARTNER'S RECOVERY

Partners: Healing From His Addiction
$14.95

Partners: Healing from His Addiction offers real hope that you can heal from his sexual addictions. After presenting statistics and personal stories, it will walk you down the path to reclaim your life, your voice, and your power, to be who you are without the impact of his addiction.

Partners Recovery Guide: 100 Empowering Exercises
$39.95

The *Partners Recovery Guide: 100 Empowering Exercises* guide was borne out of the latest in Christian self help books research on the effects on a woman who has lived with a sexual addict. This workbook will take you down the clear path of healing from the devastating impact of his sex addiction and accompany you along your entire journey.

Beyond Love: A 12 Step Guide for Partners
$14.95

Beyond Love is an interactive workbook that allows the partners of sex addicts to gain insight and strength through working the Twelve Steps. This book can be used for individual purposes or as a group study workbook.

Partner Betrayal Trauma
BOOK:$22.95/DVD:$65.95

Partner Betrayal Trauma will help you unlock that power by providing an outstanding guide on how to become stronger every day and get past the trauma of betrayal. The pain and experience of betrayal impacts all of your being and relationships. Fix your broken heart, help your relationships, and reclaim your marriage with the necessary strategies for your personal recovery.

Partner Betrayal Trauma: The Workbook
$39.95

In this workbook by Dr. Weiss, you will gain the insight and support you need to understand what betrayal trauma is and how to overcome it to be the strongest version of yourself. This is an excellent guide for those struggling to overcome the past trauma of a betrayal in their relationship.

Partner Betrayal Trauma: Step Guide
$14.95

This is an excellent step-by-step guide for those struggling to overcome the past trauma of a betrayal in their relationship. You will gain insight from a therapist who has worked with countless patients and families for over 30 years to provide them with the support they need to come out the other side whole and better versions of themselves.

He Needs To Change, Dr. Weiss
$29.95

He Needs To Change, Dr. Weiss DVD addresses the pain, trauma, and betrayal women experience because of their partner's sex addiction, betrayal, and/or intimacy anorexia. In this DVD, Dr. Weiss addresses the issue of change that he has explained to thousands of women in his office.

Unstuck for Partners
$29.95

The *Unstuck* DVD is for every woman who has experienced the pain of their partner's sex addiction or intimacy anorexia and feels stuck, confused, frustrated and unable to move on. You didn't sign up for this and honestly, you don't get it! This DVD helps you "get it" so you can process the painful reality you are in and start to live again.

Why Do I Stay, When it Doesn't make Sense
$39.95

In this video, Dr. Doug Weiss utilizes his several decades of experience to give you information and tools that can help you make your decision with mental clarity and confidence. Whether you decide to stay, separate, or divorce, your future can be filled with new opportunities and a life that you genuinely enjoy.

Triggered
$49.00

In the Triggered DVD, Dr. Weiss gives women a repertoire of tools to be successful when a trigger occurs. Triggers are normal for partners of sex addicts, but each woman's triggers are unique and must be navigated in different ways. This DVD can be a life-changing message which will validate your struggles to heal and help you face the challenges of being triggered after partner betrayal trauma.

PRODUCTS FOR INTIMACY ANOREXIA

Helping My Spouse Heal from My Intimacy Anorexia Video Course
$99.00

Are you struggling to validate your spouse's pain from Intimacy Anorexia and help them begin to heal? For the spouse of an intimacy anorexic, the pain is excruciating and sometimes even debilitating. This course is for the intimacy anorexic who is aware of their behaviors and wants to transition into a connected, intimate relationship with their spouse.

Intimacy Anorexia
BOOK:$22.95/DVD:$69.95

This hidden addiction is destroying so many marriages today. In your hands is the first antidote for someone with intimacy anorexia to turn the pages on this addiction process. Excerpts from intimacy anorexics and their spouses help this book become clinically helpful and personal in its impact to communicate hope and healing for the intimacy anorexic and the marriage.

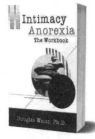

Intimacy Anorexia: The Workbook
$39.95

Intimacy Anorexia is a hidden addiction that is destryoing many marriages today. Within the pages of this workbook you will find more than 100 practical and empowering exercises to guide you through your personal recovery towards intimacy. Douglas Weiss has been successfully counseling intimacy anorexics for many years in his practice.

Intimacy Anorexia: The Steps
$14.95

This workbook follows in the tradition of the Twelve-Steps breaking down the various principles for readers so that they can experience freedom from intimacy anorexia. It is our hope that you will join the millions who have received help in their personal recovery using these Twelve-Steps.

Pain for Love
$29.95

This DVD describes in detail one of the most insidious strategies of an intimacy anorexic with their spouse. This dynamic is experienced by many who are married to an intimacy anorexic. This paradigm can empower the spouse and help them stop participating in a pain for love dynamic in their marriage.

Sin of Withholding
$49.95

This DVD is the first to address the Biblical foundation of the sin of withholding in believers' hearts. The practical application in marriage addressing Intimacy Anorexia is also interwoven in this revelational teaching on the Sin of Withholding. Once a believer is free of this sin, their walk with the Lord and their fruit towards others can increase expediently.

Narcissism Sex Addiction & Intimacy Anorexia
$29.95

The profound information that you will learn in this DVD will help you fairly evaluate your specific situation for narcissism, which will help you develop a treatment plan to address the issue you are dealing with at its core. Having this clarity can help expedite the healing process for the sex addict, intimacy anorexic, and the spouse, as they are able to tackle the real issue at hand.

Married and Alone
BOOK:$14.95/DVD:$49.95

The impact of being married and alone is very real. Dr. Weiss explains why and will help you to start a journey of recovery from living with a spouse with intimacy or sexual anorexia. My hope is that whatever reason you are watching this DVD you realize that you are worthy of being loved, whether your spouse has decided to pursue recovery or has chosen his or her anorexia over you.

Married and Alone: Healing Exercises for Spouses
$39.95

This workbook is designed to help the spouse heal from the impact of their relationship with an intimacy anorexic which may have been experienced over years or decades. The addiction patterns of an alcoholic, gambler, overeater, sex addict or intimacy anorexic have a direct impact on their spouse's life in so many ways.

Married and Alone: The Twelve Step Guide
$14.95

This book follows in the tradition of the Twelve-Steps by breaking down the various principles for each reader so that they can experience the discovery of the Twelve-Step promises. It is our hope that you will join the millions who have received help in their recovery by using these Twelve-Steps. These Steps can further your healing and recovery from your spouse's Intimacy Anorexia.

Other Resources

Worthy
WORKBOOK: $29.95/DVD$29.95

The Worthy Workbook and DVD, is designed for a 12 week study. Here is a path that anyone can take to get and stay worthy. Follow this path, and you too will make the journey from worthless to worthy just as others have.

Emotional Fitness
$16.95

Everyone has an unlimited number of emotions, but few have been trained to identify, choose, communicate, and master them. More than a guide for gaining emotional fitness and mastery, in these pages you will find a pathway to a much more fulfilling life.

Letters to My Daughter
$14.95

A gift for your daughter as she enters college. Letters to my Daughter includes my daily letters to my daughter during her first year of college. The letters are about life, God, boys, relationships and being successful in college and life in general.

Born for War
$29.95

Born for War teaches practical tools to defeat these sexual landmines and offers scriptural truths that empower young men to desire successfulness in the war thrust upon them. In this DVD, he equips this generation to win the war for their destiny. It also includes one session for parents to support their son through this battle.

Princes Take Longer Than Frogs
$29.95

This 2 hour DVD helps single women ages 15-30, to successfully navigate through the season of dating. Dr. Weiss' *Princes Take Longer Than Frogs* is a faith-based discussion broken up into several segments including Characteristics of Princes and Frogs, lies women Believe, Dating, Accountability, Boundaries, Sex and the Brain and so much more.

Indestructible
$29.95

The Indestructible series gives you a foundational understanding about your innate design as God's child. Addiction, betrayal, and abuse or neglected can all cause trials in our lives that can trigger feelings of worthlessness and defeat. God's Word reveals that your soul is not capable of being destroyed. Once you recognize and embrace your indestructible nature, you can change how you think, feel, and believe about your past, present, and future!

Sex after Recovery
$59.95

Sex after Recovery will help you navigate a variety of issues including how to reclaim a healthy sexual life together. This DVD set will help you to reclaim and recover your sexuality both individually and with each other.

Sexual Templates
$29.95

Dr. Doug Weiss, a Licensed Psychologist who has worked with thousands of men and women who are sexually addicted, have experienced trauma, or have had negative sexual experiences which have impacted their sexual template, will use his thirty years experience to help you rewire your brain and recreate a new, relational sexual template with your spouse.

I Need to Feel Safe
$29.95

This DVD provides a clear path to processing your desire for safety and creates a roadmap to reclaim safety regardless of your partner or spouse's choices. Dr. Weiss has helped thousands of women rebuild their fractured safety, heal the betrayal, and find hope for themselves. If your heart has cried out to feel safe, this DVD is a response to that heart cry.

Intrigue Addiction
$29.95

The intrigue addict is constantly on the hunt for a look or gesture from another person that insinuates they are attracted to or interested in them. The intrigue addiction can go unnoticed, but it can create just as much pain for the spouse as other sexually addictive behaviors.

Prodigal Parent Process Resources

Prodigal Parent Process
BOOK: $19.95/DVD$59.95

Dr. Weiss, drawing upon his thirty-plus years of experience working with prodigals and parents of prodigals, delivers biblical and practical tools to aid you in your journey to hope and healing. You can't change the fact that you have a prodigal but you can set your mind upon how you will go through this journey with your prodigal.

Prodigal Parent Process Workbook
$16.95

In conjunction with the Parent Prodigal Process videos and book, this workbook helps you therapeutically work through deep-rooted struggles related to being a parent of a prodigal. Working through this series and workbook will prompt serious internal dialogue with yourself as it relates to your prodigal child.

Marriage Resources

Lover Spouse
$13.95

This book provides guidelines to lead a prosperous married life and is helpful for anyone wanting to know more about what the Lord Almighty desires for your love and marriage. Featured with practical tips and foundational relationship skills, the information offered in this book will guide couples through the process of creating an intimate Christian marriage based on a solid biblical worldview.

Upgrade Your Sex Life
BOOK:$16.95/DVD:$29.95

Upgrade Your Sex Life actually teaches you own unique sexual expression that you and your partner are pre-wired to enjoy. Once you learn what your type is, you can communicate and have sex on a more satisfying level.

Servant Marriage
$13.95

Servant Marriage book is a Revelation on God's Masterpiece of marriage. In these pages, you will walk with God as He creates the man, the woman and his masterpiece called marriage.

Marriage Mondays
$59.95

This is an eight week marriage training that actually gives you the skills to have a healthy, more vibrant marriage. Each week Dr. Weiss tackles major aspects of marriage from a biblical perspective. Apply these techniques and it will transform your marriage. This course provides couples to grow their marriages either in a small group setting or as their very own private marriage retreat.

Intimacy: 100 Day Guide to a Lasting Relationship
$11.99

The *Intimacy: A 100 Day Guide to Lasting Relationships* book gives you a game plan to improve your relationships. Intimacy doesn't need to be illusive! It's time to recognize intimacy for what it is – a loving and lifelong process that you can learn and develop.

A·A·S·A·T
American Association for Sex Addiction Therapy

Sex Addiction Training Set
$1195

Both men and women are seeking to counsel more than ever for sexually addictive behaviors. You can be prepared! Forty-seven hours of topics related to sexual addiction treatment are covered in this training including:
- The Six Types of Sex Addicts
- Neurological Understanding
- Sex and Recovery
- Relapse Strategies

Partner's Recovery Training Set
$995

With this AASAT training, you will gain proven clinical insight into treating the issues facing partners. You can be prepared! Thirty-nine hours of topics related to partners treatment are covered in this training, including:
- Partner Model
- Anger
- Partner Grief
- Boundaries

Intimacy Anorexia Training Set
$995

This growing issue of Intimacy Anorexia will need your competent help in your community. Now, you can be prepared to identify it and treat it. In this training you'll cover topics like:
- Identifying Intimacy Anorexia
- Causes of Intimacy Anorexia
- Treatment Plan
- Relapse Strategies

For more information visist www.aasat.org or call 719.330.2425

Struggling with Trauma, Anxiety, and PTSD?

Trauma, anxiety, and PTSD can imbalance your brain. When your brain is out of balance, or stuck, you don't feel right and it's impossible to function at your highest level. Cereset is a proven technology that's non-invasive and highly effective. Cereset can help your brain free itself, enabling you to achieve higher levels of well-being and balance throughout your life.

Cereset – Garden of the Gods is located at Heart to Heart Counseling Center in Colorado Springs, Colorado and specializes in working with sexual addiction, intimacy anorexia, betrayal trauma, PTSD, anxiety, and more.

Here's what clients had to say about Cereset Garden of the Gods after their sessions:

"Cereset helped save our marriage. My husband and I both did Cereset and with it helping both of us be calmer and sleep better, we respond to each other in a more loving and respectful way. I notice a big change in him, and he says the same about me. After the sessions I noticed a marked improvement in my sleep and my ability to stay calm during moments that would trigger an argument with my spouse prior to Cereset. Before Cereset we felt chaotic and now, afterwards, we both feel more at peace. our household is a is a calm place to be now and we are so grateful!"

View a client
testimonial here

Schedule Your Cereset Intensive Today!

The cost for five sessions
(one per day) is $1,500.

For more information call us at 719-644-5778